SERVING UP

SERVING UP

Essays on Food, Identity and Culture

Edited by
Zoe Adjonyoh

unbound

First published in 2025

Unbound
An imprint of Boundless Publishing Group
c/o Ketton Suite, The King Centre, Main Road,
Barleythorpe, Rutland, LE15 7WD
www.unbound.com
All rights reserved

© Zoe Adjonyoh, 2025
Individual work © respective contributors, 2025

The right of Zoe Adjonyoh to be identified as the editor
of this work has been asserted in accordance with Section 77 of the Copyright,
Designs and Patents Act, 1988. No part of this publication may be copied,
reproduced, stored in a retrieval system, or transmitted, in any
form or by any means without the prior permission of the publisher, nor be
otherwise circulated in any form of binding or cover other than that in
which it is published and without a similar condition being imposed
on the subsequent purchaser.

Unbound does not have any control over, or responsibility for, any third-party
websites referred to in this book. All internet addresses given in this book were
correct at the time of going to press. The author and publisher regret any
inconvenience caused if addresses have changed or sites have ceased
to exist, but can accept no responsibility for any such changes.

Typeset in 11/14pt Adobe Garamond Pro by Jouve (UK), Milton Keynes

A CIP record for this book is available from the British Library

ISBN 978-1-80018-338-4 (paperback)
ISBN 978-1-80018-339-1 (ebook)

Printed in Great Britain by Clays Ltd, Elcograf S.p.A.

1 3 5 7 9 8 6 4 2

With special thanks to Black Food Folks for their generous support as a headline sponsor of this book

Patrons

CHEF'S ROLL
PRESENTATION IS EVERYTHING

meez

NOT 9 TO 5

BentoBox

Juliet Can – Stour Trust

The Bee Fund

Dedicated to all the 'Black Sheep' in hospitality, treading the narrow path of authenticity and commitment to a higher standard.

Contents

Foreword *Yasmin Khan*	xiii
Blending *Samah Dada*	1
Columbusing Food and What It Looks Like *Lenore T. Adkins*	7
The Food Talent Pipeline: What It Means to Develop and Train Young People in Food Media *Izzie Ramirez*	17
Un Asiento En La Mesa: Musings on Food and Cinema *Yoshivel Elise Chirinos*	31
'It's too spicy' and Other Such Bullshit *Fatima 'Fatti' Tarkleman*	43
The Things We Could Not Swallow: On 'Good' Taste, Identity and Grief *Cynthia Greenlee*	49
Eating Our Feelings: The Role of Food in Death Rituals, and How It Helps Us Process Loss *Tiffani Rozier*	59
Inheritance *Apoorva Sripathi*	65
Still Standing: Field Notes on Removed Confederate Statues *Duron Chavis*	73
Serving Up Sisterhood: The Power of Black Feminism, Food and Freedom *Tambra Raye Stevenson, MPH, MA*	81
Neuro Spicy: Overlooked and Undervalued, the Dismissal of ADHD Traits in the Workplace *Zoe Adjonyoh*	91

CONTENTS

Psychological Safety in Hospitality and Beyond *Hassel Aviles*	107
I Am Not Safe If My Whole Self Is Not Safe *Vanessa Parish*	119
Hamantaschen *Abigail Koffler*	125
Was Anthony Bourdain Wrong About Vegan Food? *Lee Tran Lam*	133
Eatplaces: Tables Talk of Yesterdays *Scott Alves Barton*	145
Why Black Spaces Are Needed in an Industry That Refuses to Change *Selasie Dotse*	157
Find Your People *Mavis-Jay Sanders*	165
Your Hands Look Different Now *Chris Nigro*	173
Afterword *Zoe Adjonyoh*	177
About the Authors	179
Acknowledgements	189
Notes	191
Supporters	199

Foreword

When I first had the idea of using food stories to challenge stereotypes of how people from the Muslim world are perceived in the West, I think it's fair to say my friends raised an eyebrow or two. As Toni Morrison says, 'All good art is political! There is none that isn't. And the ones that try hard not to be political are political by saying, "We love the status quo." '[1] My life up until that point had been focused on grassroots activism: working for non-profits, trade unions and small campaign groups, campaigning for racial justice and police accountability but also mobilising against Western military interventions in the Middle East and corporate profiteering from war. Fair play to my mates, these were hardly topics that a new recipe for hummus were going to resolve.

But here's the thing.

Stories matter. Voices matter. Representation matters.

Social narratives are political constructs, too often created and curated in today's society for the benefit of a privileged few. The way we perceive food culture is a product of these wider societal narratives. The hospitality industry and food media are no different to any other part of contemporary society – they carry with them the residue of centuries of imperialism, colonialism and capitalist hegemony. In order to evolve towards a more just and equitable society for all, we need to open up the space to discuss how these industries might be decolonised, deconstructed and – most importantly – reimagined. As the Kenyan analyst Joe Kobuthi noted, 'food has always been a fundamental tool in the process of colonization. Through food, social and cultural norms are conveyed and also violated.'[2] Today, the legacy of this plays out not only in who gets to talk, write and cook the food we eat, but also how we each experience the multitude of diverse culinary traditions that exist in this world.

For me, this has meant spending much of the last decade researching and writing cookbooks that celebrate the power of the human spirit in countries more commonly associated with conflict. I've heard and shared stories about the resilience and resistance of Palestinian farmers in the West Bank protecting their olive groves from destruction by Israeli settlers, and observed the strength and grace of artisan chocolatiers in Tehran who are defying crushing US sanctions to share beauty in the confectionery they make. I have traversed the island of Cyprus, exploring how the legacy of British colonialism has led to divided kitchens on the historical island, but I have also spent time with the volunteer-run food initiatives supporting refugees in Greece, and questioned whether solidarity through food might help us imagine a world without borders.

FOREWORD

I do this because it's always been clear to me that when we talk about food, we are describing so much more than a simple set of ingredients. To explore what we find on our plates is to take a snapshot of a cultural moment in time. The food we eat tells us stories about history, trade, empire, economics, gender relations, agriculture, the climate crisis and culture. A good recipe can read like a good story, and it can shape narratives through a medium we can all relate to: a really good meal.

All of this is why I was so excited to dive into this diverse collection of essays, skilfully edited by Zoe Adjonyoh, a ground-breaking thought leader who has stood at the forefront of the movement to decolonise Western food media. What follows on these pages is a selection of thought-provoking and moving essays which curiously and passionately examine concepts of ownership, representation, cultural appropriation, class, economic disparity, health, and food security. I hope that these stories serve up both debate and discussion at your dining table and inspire you to think, act and perhaps even cook differently.

Yasmin Khan
November 2023

Blending

Samah Dada

I've been thinking about blending a lot. Sauces, fillings, soups. To mix and combine until the constituent parts are indistinguishable. Makes sense for a smoothie. Not so much for me.

But I tried.

I have been trying to blend in for most of my life, though I'm not sure I've been that good at it. There has always been a part of me resistant to the blades, unwilling to become something that ultimately I am not.

I've spent most of my life trying to achieve that smoothness. The ease of being twirled along into an existence of uniformity. Everything coming together, as if there were no parts at all, just the sum. Fitting in. Belonging.

My parents immigrated to the United States when they

were in high school. They brought much of their Indian heritage with them, but not quite enough to make me feel like their roots could unquestionably belong to me too. While I had the traditional clothes, a knowledge of customs and practices, and reminders of my family through frequent calls to India, the puzzle pieces didn't quite seem to fit. What did belong to me, though, was the feeling that I didn't. Growing up I had friends, but it was obvious that I didn't look like (nor was I like) the other kids in school. I didn't know another family with immigrant parents – everyone seemed to have had the same upbringing, except me. Though I was – and am – extremely proud of my heritage, I felt a need to hide it to make my existence more palatable for the Western community I was ingrained into.

Mine is not a new story, it's the immigrant one. Sukha gosht sandwiches were eventually swapped for Nutella ones, alongside Lunchables and Pop-Tarts. Like everyone else.

But the thing is, I wasn't like everyone else – no matter how hard I tried. I didn't feel desi enough, though the gorgeous Indian dinner spreads placed on the table by my mom every night would try their best to exclaim, loudly, otherwise. But I also didn't feel American – I was consistently othered by my peers, my name was made fun of, and the 'Where are you from?' question floated above my head everywhere I went.

Feeling different from others at such a young age, despite my parents' successful assimilation, instilled the seed of a notion that planted itself within me and grew well into my adult years – that my worth was dependent on how well I could fit into a mould. Challenge accepted, I guess.

Throughout my life I've been very good at trying. Effort

was never an issue for me. In fact, I've pretty much been an A+ student at it, if I may say so myself. If you keep trying you'll get there, right? Truth is, I've been good at trying to fit in but not very great at succeeding at it. Which is annoying for someone who has spent a great deal of her life trying to be perfect at everything she could.

I struggled to find myself in the people I saw on my favourite television shows or in the books I read, so I revelled in a Princess Jasmine Halloween costume that I wore (read: rocked) for five years straight simply because I saw a little bit of myself represented in her. My cultural differences were only put on display during International Day events at school, where I was finally able to don my traditional garb and pass out jalebi or gulab jamun to my peers. Or, when I celebrated Eid, with henna covering my hands, having the opportunity to explain that – it's sort of like your Christmas? But though I didn't feel like I belonged in California, India still felt foreign to me. I understand more Urdu than I speak – and am shy about practising because my American accent and Western mannerisms rarely give me the confidence to even try.

This cultural balancing act of mine has historically bestowed upon me the determination to be the most accommodating human on earth. I could be a people-pleaser to make up for all I felt that I could not be. I thought my perfectionistic tendencies would mask my differences and paint them over with praiseworthy pigment. At the time I found this tiring, but I know now that I have accidentally turned my people-pleasing into palate-pleasing, converting my weakness into my strength. Cooking is the passion of my life, and nothing brings me closer to myself than pleasing the palates of others (and my own, too).

Despite my lack of belonging in every other aspect of life, dinner always felt different. It was almost like I had been programmed to eat dal and rice with my hands, scoop up my mom's chana masala with roti and declare with reckless abandon that my favourite food was biryani. I didn't have to code switch to belong here. I jumped at any opportunity to watch my mom cook, peering over the stove to speculate how each dish she threw together, sans measuring spoons and cups, came out completely perfect each time. Everything was methodical, but hardly precise. I always used to wonder, how can she replicate this if she doesn't even know what was added in the first place?

Whenever I'd pepper my mom with these insistent queries, she would always quip that a dish never really turns out exactly the same each time she makes it. Sometimes she'll add this, sometimes she'll add that. While we all know that there are many circumstances in which cooking or baking can and should be exacting, I learned from my mother to trust my andaaz, which in Hindi translates to your own style and estimation. And that, to me, is one of the best, most beautiful parts of the art of cooking – you iterate, and change, and try new things until you surprise even yourself.

Though my mom would cook multiple dishes a night, she was never in the kitchen all day. She has always had a particular style of Indian cooking; her dishes are a little lighter and brighter, frequently vegetable-focused, without using dairy or exorbitant amounts of oil. In a similar way, my style of cooking is what I like to call accidentally plant-based. I never set out to make my recipes fall into a specific diet or lifestyle. But much of my work happens to be vegetarian, vegan, gluten-free and dairy-free. I choose not to lead with these labels because they can seem clinical or reductive (I mean let's face it, nobody calls carrots 'vegan carrots').

The truth is, my recipes represent the ways you can be creative with a short list of minimal and whole ingredients. It's about doing more with less. Of course I love sharing that the soft and chewy cookie you just ate was mainly made up of almonds, coconut, maple syrup and dates. Or that the creamy pasta you just took a bite of had no cream at all, but was instead made using ripe avocados, basil and olive oil. It can be fun to share new ways of eating, but it's more than that. The fact that my recipes can be relished by individuals who never thought they could enjoy a gluten-free brownie or a slice of dairy-free carrot cake represents the inclusivity I chase in every aspect of my work. It's one of my greatest motivators and sources of pride.

While my mom's cooking has always inspired me, it's my own cooking that has led me back to myself. Maybe it has even led me to myself, to my immigrant roots for the first time. Nothing in my life has ever made more sense to me. I have connected well with other people my entire life. But the kitchen is the first place where I've been able to connect with myself.

Cooking has allowed me to express who I am in ways that young Samah was always afraid to and wouldn't believe. For me, it is not just a means to an end, a process carried out in the kitchen with the sole purpose of satisfying an inherent human need. It is art. And I can be loud with my paint. Hands as brushes, playing with new ingredients as colours, exploring all the ways in which I can create and iterate and change – the kitchen is the first place where I gave myself permission to abandon perfection, make mistakes, and as a result, accept who I am, fully. It's the language with which I can express myself better.

I find parts of myself in the edges of an 8x8 brownie pan as much as I do in the depths of a steaming, creamy, hearty bowl of dal. I marry dates and nut butters like I am the best officiant around (but I think I knew they were soulmates from the start). Confidence in the kitchen has allowed me to have it in every other aspect of my life. It has given me the courage to show off my heritage on my plate and within the pan, instead of tucking it away because of the fear that I won't be accepted. Food is connection, it is love, it is energy, it is messy, it is beautiful. This art can imitate life.

I know this sounds dramatic – that maybe I've found my purpose in life, or that I know who I am. I love that you might think that. But I think who I am – and who you are – evolves silently, loudly, and as often as we want. I am not the same as I was ten years ago or yesterday. I won't be the same tomorrow. And this revelation has allowed me to reframe my life.

I used to ask myself, who am I? Where do I fit in? I guess what I should have been asking myself is, how can I stand out?

How can I make my flavours and my recipes bolder? How do I create a sense of belonging if I can't find it in others? How can I innovate and innovate, and fail and fail, and succeed (what does this even mean, anyway?) again and again? And then again?

I'm glad I didn't figure out how to blend the different parts of myself into an agreeable, smooth mixture. Each ingredient, each part of myself, always deserved to sing loudly, even if I didn't realise it at the time. After all, only those unique ingredients can create a dish that is distinctly, unapologetically me.

Columbusing Food and What It Looks Like

Lenore T. Adkins

A middle-aged white man wearing a red, yellow and green Rastafarian tam complete with fake dreadlocks dangling down his back caught my attention as his open-air tour bus pulled away.

I was in Saint Thomas, a United States territory and former British colony. And I could not understand why this tourist was wearing something that's rooted in Black, Jamaican culture. Was he mocking the locals? Does he know what a Rastafarian is? Does he realise that Black people sometimes have difficulty securing jobs when we wear our hair in its natural state? Did he care? Or was this just a cute wig for him to wear in 'paradise' and take off once he returned home?

I am constantly navigating my own Blackness, to the point where if I'm wearing braids or dreads, I'll wear my hair down when I pass through airport security. This is so that security personnel won't search my hair. In one case, I was terrified of alienating a new white friend by talking about a racist incident, so I thought about watering it down. In the end, I gave it to him straight, and he wasn't offended. We're constantly bending and negotiating our existence and thinking about white people's feelings. Meanwhile, many pick and choose from our culture, make money from it and don't give us a second thought.

Cultural appropriation comes in many different forms. But at its core, it involves the dominant culture stealing from, altering and/or profiting off the people and cultures that society has systematically excluded and institutionally oppressed.

In food, it often happens when people who have zero connection to a culture find ways to make money off it. I have been a food writer since 2017 and see far too much of this behaviour happening and far too many people in the white-dominated food media looking the other way.

Earlier this year, I found out that an expensive, white-owned, Michelin-starred restaurant in Washington was playing loud, hardcore rap music, complete with the N-word and misogynistic language including 'bitch'. They played it during dinner service, despite multiple complaints, some from prominent food critics and African American customers.

The white male chef-owner and two of his white male executives at this rarefied restaurant had curated a twenty-two-hour playlist for its mostly white patrons that was dominated by explicit versions of songs from Kanye West, Jay-Z, Drake, Kendrick Lamar and others. A good friend of mine called this 'audio blackface'.

The restaurant does not serve Black cuisine, so there is no culinary connection to this music. A Black chef playing this music in his Michelin-starred restaurant would be accused of alienating white customers.

One of the people who complained, a Black woman who is also an eye doctor, showed me a written response from the restaurant, which called the language 'provocative', 'loaded' and themselves a 'youthful team' that 'often toe the line of experimentation and risqué content'. They apologised for not being more cognisant of how the music affected the woman's dinner and assured her that 'we have taken your words very seriously'.

Except they didn't. For at least another year, they were still playing the same offensive tunes.

Elsewhere, there was Lucky Lee's, the Chinese restaurant in New York City that closed after eight months in 2019. Social media users denounced its owner Arielle Haspel, a white, female nutritionist, for profiting off the culture as she denigrated it, according to the *New York Times*.[1]

She promoted her riff on Chinese food as 'clean', and less 'oily', 'salty' and 'icky' than the Chinese cuisine you're used to, the *New York Times* reported. This feeds into racist stereotypes about American Chinese food and restaurants being dirty, unhealthy and gross.

Social media users didn't stop there. According to the *New York Times* they also lambasted the owner over the restaurant's name, which implied a Chinese person owned it. 'Lee' was the name of Haspel's white husband. *Eater New York* reported that the Chinese food the Jewish couple ate growing up in New York City inspired the wife to open the restaurant.

I have questions. What kind of research did the owners do before opening Lucky Lee's, and who are they to decide that Chinese food needs an update? Did the owners realise that Chinese immigrants in the United States invented what we call 'Chinese food' and have been tailoring it to white-American tastes for more than a hundred years? General Tso's chicken, orange chicken, egg rolls, chop suey and more were all invented in the United States. So were those ubiquitous white takeout containers. In other words, the Chinese food in this country is already Americanised.

Writing for *Eater New York*, Esther Tseng reported:

> Their recipes were adapted for the American palate – for instance, adding sugar and frying more items – creating a new culinary genre in the process. And because Chinatowns were considered 'slums', Chinese food acquired its still-present reputation as dirty. That needs to be acknowledged and respected in its historical context: American Chinese food evolved into what it is today because white people were its primary audience.[2]

Taking a step back, there were more than 24,000 Chinese restaurants in the United States in 2023, a 1.2 per cent increase from 2022, according to IBISWorld.[3] Did the owners ever wonder why this is the case? Basically, a loophole in the Chinese Exclusion Act of 1882 – a law that suspended Chinese immigration and made it difficult for legal residents to re-enter the United States – let some business owners in if they secured 'merchant status' by opening a restaurant. This special status let Chinese business owners travel to China and bring employees back with them to the United States.

Tyra Wu writes for *Spoon University*:

> Obtaining a merchant visa was difficult and only the major investors of 'high-end' restaurants qualified. To subvert this rule, Chinese immigrants would pool their money to start luxury 'chop-suey' restaurants, taking turns running the restaurant for a year or so. Once they obtained merchant status, they would use it to bring over family members to work in the restaurant.[4]

This prompted the number of American Chinese restaurants to grow exponentially in the early part of the twentieth century.

This sector of the industry is booming, which is what attracts cultural appropriation from people like Arielle Haspel. But excuses and apologies from white restaurant owners often miss the mark. What the affronted culture needs is respect.

In 2017, the Chicago chain Aloha Poke Co. issued an apology on Facebook to Native Hawaiians after its attorneys sent cease-and-desist letters demanding that raw fishbowl businesses in the US with the words 'poke' and 'aloha' in their names alter their branding. Aloha and poke are integral parts of Hawaiian culture and pre-date the Chicago-based chain by hundreds of years.

Poke (pronounced 'po-kay') bowls are a staple of Hawaiian cuisine. A traditional poke bowl is filled with white rice and topped with raw fish that's been marinated in green onions, sesame oil, soy sauce and various spices. It's usually made with ahi tuna, but you could also use salmon, cooked shrimp or tofu.

Poke means 'to slice' in Hawaiian. Native Hawaiians previously cut up smaller reef fish and served them raw. But when Japanese immigrants started arriving in the late 1800s to work on Hawaii's sugarcane plantations, ahi tuna became the poke fish of choice. Poke bowls with rice fuse Hawaiian flavours with Japanese donburi and have been a mainstay in restaurants in Hawaii for the past three decades, according to the *Washington Post*.[5]

Despite this long history, *Eater Chicago* reported that the attorneys' cease-and-desist letters came as the Chicago-based chain eyed a national expansion. Some letters, *Eater Chicago* reported, targeted family-owned restaurants that local and Native Hawaiians own in their home state.[6]

The apology followed a social media backlash in which users posted negative restaurant reviews and comments on Facebook and Yelp and planned a national boycott against the company.

The company's 490-word *mea culpa* on its Facebook account apologised to 'those who care very passionately about their Hawaiian culture', and attempted to set the record straight about the company.

> What we have done is attempted to stop trademark infringers in the restaurant industry from using the trademark 'Aloha Poke' without permission. This is a very common practice used across industries, and, in particular, the restaurant industry to protect the use of a business' name and brand.[7]

At least one restaurant changed their name after they received the attorneys' cease-and-desist letters. The Aloha Poke

Shop was a poke restaurant and Hawaiian general store in Anchorage, Alaska that Tasha Kahele, a Native Hawaiian, and her family opened in 2014. Their family business opened two years before the Chicago-based chain, who gave the family roughly two months to change the name of its shop to something else, *Eater Chicago* reported.[8]

They settled on the name Lei's Poke Shop, in homage to their eldest daughter, Leihoku, a part-owner who has helped run the business since 2015. The process meant paying for a new logo, signage and reaching out to the local health department. The family felt pressured into obeying the cease-and-desist letter because of the chain's deep pockets.

'We cannot financially afford to go up against those guys,' Kahele told *Eater Chicago*. 'We had no choice but to comply, which has caused much financial stress and hardships for the family.'

Levy Family Partners, along with Mark Lawrence, founder and chief executive officer of SpotHero, invested millions of dollars into the Chicago chain for its national expansion. To date, it has expanded to major cities, including Washington, Miami, and smaller cities in Minnesota and Texas. Things have changed for the family-owned business since then, and it too is expanding. In 2021, it opened a second location in Wasilla, Alaska.

That the company thought to trademark words that aren't even theirs after appropriating and making money off a dish that they didn't originate is baffling. This triggered many Hawaiians because it represented another front in their ongoing fight to preserve their cultural heritage and autonomy in the United States, which many still see as an invader. Hawaii was an independent kingdom before the US colonised it in the late 1800s (it became the fiftieth state in 1959). And for almost a century, from 1896 until 1987, Hawaiians were forbidden from using their native language in the public schools.

Dr Kalamaokaaina Niheu, a Native Hawaiian activist, released a Facebook video that accused the company of cultural appropriation and called on the Hawaiian diaspora and allies to protest outside of the company's Chicago headquarters. The video promptly went viral and ignited anger on social media among locals who won't stand for outsiders policing their language.

'In the language there is life and in the language there is death,' Niheu said in the video. 'So if we let these people, these businessmen take the word "Aloha" from us, and illegalize it by our own people, we are complicit in our own destruction of our history, we are complicit in . . . the erasure of our people and we are complicit in allowing these people to harass and subjugate and oppress our people.'[9]

There are times, though, when the media fails to hold alleged cultural appropriators accountable.

Liz 'LC' Connelly, one of two white women owners of the now-shuttered Kooks Burritos, confessed to a reporter that she and her then business partner, Kali Wilgus, essentially stole their tortilla-making method from Mexican women. This spiralled from Connelly's and Wilgus' 2016 vacation to Puerto Nuevo, Mexico during Christmas, the season of giving.

'I picked the brains of every tortilla lady there . . . and they showed me a little of what they did,' Connelly told a reporter from the *Willamette Week*.[10] 'They wouldn't tell us too much about technique, but we were peeking into the windows of every kitchen.'

Connelly described the handmade flour tortillas that wrapped around her $5 lobster in a burrito as 'stretchy and a little buttery, and best of all, unlimited'.

Months after their Mexican holiday, according to the article, Connelly and Wilgus used what they took from the women and their own recipe guesswork to open Kooks Burritos: a weekend breakfast burrito pop-up inside a taco cart located in a trendy part of Southern Portland.

Some people, I'm sure, would say this was genius.

But there's so much to unpack here. I'm not sure I understand why the former owners thought they could travel to another country with the expectation that the locals would spill their culinary secrets to them without financial compensation. And when it was clear the tortilla makers weren't comfortable with divulging detailed information about their methods, the business owners didn't stop there. They were so hellbent on cracking the tortilla code that they spied on the locals without their consent, secured unauthorised intel about the women's technique, returned to the United States, and made money from their unethical information gathering.

Then they bragged about their exploits to a local reporter at the *Willamette Week*, who, from the looks of the resulting review, did not ask uncomfortable questions about colonisation, the women's unethical behaviour, or why the women felt like they should make these tortillas and serve these burritos. What also wasn't asked: how the women secured financing for their pop-up so fast – they opened it months after their Mexican holiday – and why they named their business Kooks. In surfing parlance, kooks are posers. The review served as a glorified press release for Kooks and appeared to endorse their questionable behaviour.

Instead, the pushback came from the public. Comments on the story exploded, with many accusing the women of cultural appropriation, while others came to their defence or bashed the newspaper.

One online commenter said the article was a clear example of how media perpetuates and reinforces racism and white supremacy, brandishing it as fun and innovative.

Two days after the *Willamette Week* published its review, the women shut their business down amid the uproar, pointing to several death threats they received, the newspaper reported. Local, national and international media ran with the story, blowing it up further and turning it into a viral piece of clickbait.

As food writers, it is our job to hold restaurant owners accountable and shine a light on injustice, not churn out stenography or normalise obvious exploitation. We should be thinking about the people who did all of the culinary legwork and who are being ignored and/or demonised while others profit from their culture and labour. We are supposed to be sceptical and ask the hard questions, not take what people say at face value.

If food writers can't do this, they may as well join the restaurants' PR team. If food media operates without honesty and integrity, there will be no one left, aside from the public, to hold cultural appropriators accountable.

The Food Talent Pipeline: What It Means to Develop and Train Young People in Food Media

Izzie Ramirez

Writing has the power to shape how we perceive the world. With a quick turn of phrase, I could convince you that, yes, you really should go to that new coffee shop across the street. Or that it's a mistake to vote for the politician everyone's swooning over. I might craft a particularly compelling narrative that rattles your entire mindset. But the writer is not the only one who has power.

Editors and producers within publishers and media companies act as cultural gatekeepers: they make decisions about what writers should care about and why. As an editor myself, I'm very familiar with the day-to-day decisions we might think are minor, but have long-lasting ramifications. We interpret events and prescribe meaning to them. We lop off paragraphs we think are unnecessary in favour of ones that feel more entertaining or enlightening. For decades now, decision-makers within these fields have prioritised the voices of cis, white writers to dictate how we should think about food.

That's partially reflective of the American news industry as a whole. According to a 2018 Pew Research Center analysis of US Census Bureau data from 2012 to 2016, more than three-quarters of newsroom employees* (77 per cent) were non-Hispanic whites.[1] Newsroom managers were even whiter; 81 per cent were white in a diversity survey conducted by the American Society of News Editors in 2018. The numbers are even more stark in terms of gender; women make up one third of newsrooms overall, men are overrepresented and trans and nonbinary people are often not even included in surveys.[2]

While race and gender do not preclude someone from writing about identities other than their own, the reality is that how we move in the world informs how we write. As with all writing, it's impossible to remove yourself from your work; our fingerprints leave traces everywhere we go. No, I do not think 'neutral' or 'objective' writing is possible – but that we should try to evaluate facts and our opinions as thoroughly as possible. We shouldn't get sloppy. For food media specifically, myopic decision-making from white editors and writers alike has serious consequences. Not only does it set a standard for others to only write about topics close to them, but it also influences the general public's understanding of which foods matter. 'Matter' here can have several

---

* Newsroom employees include reporters, editors, photographers, videographers, etc. Anyone who produces work in the news industry.

definitions: what's delicious, what's cool, what's healthy, what's spiritual, or what's important.

But food cannot be removed from our lived experiences. From gochugaru and epazote to long-and-slow barbecuing and lively fermenting, our food tells us where we are from, what our ancestors made, and what we choose to share. As children, our tastes develop according to what we're exposed to in our homes and in our communities. These are not the only reasons, but they do play a role. Other factors include the income of the parents and genetics, among others.[3] It's partially why I'm not inclined to cook with pickles or dill, but I gravitate towards fire-breathing spice and bright flavours.* Growing up in a Mexican-Puerto Rican household in suburbs outside Baltimore and Dallas has led me to have a very specific point of view when it comes to food. Importantly, there is nothing wrong with having preferences – but it becomes a problem when it impacts one's ability to write about a different cuisine with respect. What's worse is that if you can't see another's cuisine as deserving of appreciation or intrigue, you tend to dehumanise and alienate entire groups of people along the way.

In June 2020, I wrote for Bitch Media about the fallout from food magazine *Bon Appétit*'s explosive internal problems, when the George Floyd protests facilitated talks about equity within the company. Employees of colour were not being paid as much as their white counterparts to star in viral

---

* No hate to these foods! I promise I'm coming around. Really into tzatziki and pickled onions right now – ten-year-old me would be shocked.

YouTube videos, and yet, their presence was integral to showing how 'cultured' the magazine has become. Look! We know what sumac is! That's on top of the embarrassing news that the publication's editor-in-chief, Adam Rapoport, postured as a Puerto Rican for a Halloween years before refusing to accept pitches about Puerto Rican food.[4] Back then, my takeaway was that it shouldn't have taken people of colour overworking in trendy videos for audiences to see the value in learning and trying new-to-you foods. At the time, I was working as a freelancer and it emphasised my frustrations at the Schrödinger's Cat situation I found myself in: simultaneously, everyone and no one wanted me to write about Hispanic foods. Editors were desperate to diversify their articles in the wake of the protests, but only had their eyes on stories that affirmed pre-existing narratives of diversity. The same is true anytime those heritage months roll around. But that support disappears when the clock strikes midnight. The brownface portion of the news cycle was an additional fuck you.

Despite how all-encompassing the *Bon Appétit* scandal was, unsurprisingly, little has changed since. Hell, literally during the same month, the *New York Times* ran an egregious article by Hannah Beech titled 'Eating Thai Fruit Demands Serious Effort but Delivers Sublime Reward'.[5] Throughout the piece, Beech complains about how all these fruits were too much work, and that she didn't really vibe with the flavours. 'Unlike a banana's easy extraction, dissecting a jackfruit is to hack through a jagged sheath, then painstakingly pluck out rubbery polyps that taste like overripe Juicy Fruit gum,' she writes. I find it hard to believe she would describe raspberries – which are equally as polyp-like, may

I add! – the same way. Let me emphasise: it's not just the writer who is at fault here. An editor also allowed such work to slide. Decisions were made at every step of the way. It's not an accident.

To be clear, this is not a new problem; poor editorial oversight impacts every single vertical at every publication. Conversations regarding the diversification of newsrooms and the work we publish have been going on for decades long before 2020, and progress is being made slowly but surely. However, there hasn't been a 180-degree shift when it comes to maintaining employees of colour. The George Floyd protests certainly put a light under the asses of several publications, and as a result they've moved to hire more writers of colour, but as the years go on, the maintenance efforts have fallen short. These employees are often underpaid and their performance undervalued* in comparison to their white counterparts, as seen by several newsrooms' unionisation efforts.[6] Anecdotally, more and more employees of colour are burning out and leaving the industry. The pressure to produce work that represents entire communities while not being given the editorial leeway or support to produce those stories has led to a tension within newsrooms. In my opinion, that's because most managers do not recognise that hires alone will not fix the historical, systemic problems that haunt newsroom dynamics.

---

* In 2022, the *New York Times*' union conducted a survey of 1,000 members and found the following: 'Being Hispanic reduced the odds of receiving a high score by about 60 per cent, and being Black cut the chances of high scores by nearly 50 per cent.'

In the last few years, I've climbed the corporate ladder in the media world, so to speak. I've always been a mentor to young writers of colour in my free time, but only in the last few years have I had the opportunity to do so as a full-time, salaried employee. I am not going to pretend that I have all the answers, or that I'm a Diversity, Equity and Inclusion pro. In fact, this essay isn't going to touch DEI initiatives at all. That's not to say that DEI isn't important or valuable, but that it isn't enough, in my experience. Most DEI trainings focus on learning about bias when making hiring decisions or the treatment of your direct reports from a human resources lens. That's huge for people who have never learned terms like equity, microaggresions, and so on and so forth. But rarely do these initiatives interrogate the consequences of bad, inadequate storytelling that perpetuates the very harms we're trying to eliminate intrapersonally in the office. Nor, in my experience, do DEI programmes challenge salary inequality or other structural issues that impact performance transparently.*

So, what would it mean to shift that structure to be more inclusive? It's not just about changing the folks in the C-suite or replacing editors. Working to uplift young BIPOC, LGBTQ+ people is key to seeing food media that truly reflects us. That said, it requires us in the middle to revitalise publications and institutions to help support the skills and

---

* Sometimes, I laugh about how a former employer hired a DEI specialist who conducted a survey that did not reveal anything about pay for employees by gender, race and level of experience. It was just a formal pat on the back.

development of young folks better while also dismantling the systemic issues at play that squash creativity, diversity and ingenuity.

In the Middle

I'm going to immediately contradict myself. Middle managers *shouldn't* have to be the movers and shakers within a company. It's undue, additional pressure. However, if you care about the careers of your direct reports, it's a necessity to advocate for them – even if it means putting yourself at odds with your superiors. But there are smaller and equally as impactful ways to set up your writers for success, regardless of the identities they hold. (I'm writing from my experiences as an editor in digital media, but these practices could extend far beyond to other industries, like hospitality and marketing.)

The first, of course, is pay. Hopefully, you were transparent about salary, benefits and union eligibility during the hiring process.* If you weren't able to be for whatever reason, the next best move is to track your employees' wins. Yes, you're going to do your mid-cycle and end-of-year performance reviews, but realistically it's much easier to forget the

---

* In some states, it's required to list the starting salary in job descriptions. Also, in the year of our Lord 2025, it's embarrassing to not list the salary. If your employer is hesitant to give you this information, show them the Writers of Color Twitter account, which drags those who post jobs without transparency. Additionally, I've only ever had success as an employer when I share salary! We receive more applicants. Not being honest is shooting yourself in the foot.

good stuff and linger on the bad. Everyone has a different system for this – I personally like using a spreadsheet – but what matters here is that you can put numbers for impact (maybe it's pageviews, engaged minutes, circulation on social media, changing a law, awards, etc.). Be wary of obsession and arbitrary metrics. Tracking is only meant for you to be able to have hard data that's palatable to upper management when you're trying to get someone a raise.

If you're unable to pay employees what they deserve, the next best course of action is to fight for a larger discretionary budget for projects and professional development. You have to forge opportunities for creativity so your team can stretch and grow. Buzzy, career-making packages and features require time and therefore money. Sure, you can write stories about anywhere without having to leave your living room, but the most intimate, touching pieces are the ones that take you to an abuela's kitchen to knead the masa yourself, to taste the mole, to feel her time-worn hands over yours. The prose naturally follows. The tragic part is getting to that house might require a train ticket, a photographer at a day rate, and several hours that could be spent on other projects. As a manager, though, those logistics are your problem, not your direct reports'. Collaborate with them and upper management to figure out what's possible, and work from there.

As for more specific professional development, ask your direct reports what and how they'd like to grow. It may be that they want to take a wine-tasting class so they can become a better wine reporter; or maybe they want to connect with other journalists who share their same identity. Conferences and classes can be expensive, especially if there's travel involved, so working with your superiors to create an annual budget can help offset the costs on your team. If your staffer is underpaid, use that as ammo: 'Well, X can't afford the $500 conference fee because we don't pay them enough – this is the least we can do. It'll also help improve the content we produce in these ways . . .'

Let's say you've already acquired an incredible professional development budget and you've been able to give them decent end-of-year bonuses or a salary bump that evens out differences on your team. From here, you should start thinking about consistent, cross-skill trainings. As a manager, your job is to build your staffers and stretch them. If they've never done an investigative piece that requires public record requests, set up a training with someone within the company who can walk them through the Freedom of Information Act. You could also connect your team to other professionals or academics who work in tangential fields so they can see their beats in a new way. Have them study other writers critically and analyse what works and what doesn't. Remember: not every employee will have received formal education. It's common for writers of colour to not go to journalism school! And you know what – they shouldn't need to in order to succeed in a newsroom. Make sure they have the skills to succeed no matter where they go. Editors must take the time to fill in the gaps and always keep learning. Together.

Lastly, you want to foster an environment where your direct reports can come to you when they have concerns about their work or about the newsroom. Feedback is crucial to operating a team that can see itself clearly. If a writer cannot express their worry about how an edit may come off as ableist, or if they feel unsafe in team meetings because a co-worker insists on making inappropriate jokes, everyone loses. Comfort is not about letting inadequate or problematic things slide because it makes you uneasy. Comfort is trust.

The Writing Itself

When working with young writers, especially if they are new to journalism and its conventions, recognise that they are going to have a tonne of moral questions relating to objectivity, activism, inclusion of self and privacy. These questions should be asked! Just because historically stories were written in a certain way, it doesn't mean it *always* has to be done that way. I think a lot about Indigenous perceptions of time and Latine methods of storytelling – when a feature piece allows, I try to play with the structure, for instance. Never ignore a writer's desire to play with form, but do clue them in on why specific editorial choices have to be made. Sometimes, you need the no-nonsense 800-word news story to go up today.

Of course, every editorial decision is a moral one. That can be scary for new writers of colour or LGBTQ+ writers. Paralysing, even. I've seen situations where writers freeze and can't produce out of fear of doing a community wrong (I've been there myself in graduate school!). But what ends up happening is self-sabotage. An inability to make a narrative choice – a requirement for storytelling – leads to work that is fractured and does right by no one. Not the reader, not the communities covered, and certainly not the writer. Partially the issue stems from a lack of confidence. It takes time to build that.

As for the work that makes it to print or the web, there are several ways to build 'checks' for yourself and for your writers. It's impossible to be attuned to every stereotype or know every context, but that doesn't mean we should become lazy or careless. The writer should be responsible for: finding diverse, knowledgeable sources; backgrounding and uncovering context; situating the news element well; crafting a narrative that makes sense to an outsider, without alienating or othering the insider; and light fact-checking.* Editors, of which there should be several, should interrogate said narrative and also question where the story fits within the larger scope of work produced about the topic. (Honestly, some of that work should be done at the assigning and pitching stage. Example: maybe instead of accepting a tired pitch about how much work Asian fruits are, you assign a story about why fruit sellers do what they do.)

From an editorial perspective, the biggest trap editors fall into is thinking that just because a writer has a certain identity or background, that they are an automatic expert on everything about said topic, country, place or cuisine. Sure, it's helpful to be a bit more familiar. And it can be smarter to assign, say, a Hispanic writer to a story about the Latine diaspora than a white writer. I can see why that's valuable. But, your writer may actually not be familiar with the third-generation diaspora at all because they're an immigrant!

---

* Sources do not have to be scholarly experts to be able to bring something to the table. Often, when we rely only on academics, we tend to only quote white people. That's because academia is disproportionately white (similarly to journalism, academics are underpaid, which really only allows those with outside support to be able to survive and progress in the field).

Some writers of colour and LGBTQ+ writers may only want to write about their own communities, and that's perfectly fine. A win, in my opinion. But to pigeonhole them is inappropriate and extremely short-sighted. Exclusion because of identity or experience, similarly, is wrong. Assign writers according to their interests – which they must back up with expertise and an eye for their own biases – and the work will speak for itself.

Maintenance Also Means Looking Out for You

If you also happen to be an editor of colour or an LGBTQ+ one, it will be exhausting constantly having to fight for the best outcomes for your team when, systemically, you, too, are at the whims of those who may not understand where you're coming from. You're expected to maintain the status quo, make the most money possible for the company and often with minimal resources. Somehow, you'll find yourself doing more work for your pieces, whether it be because of sensitivity reads or because you're seen as 'representative' of a group. We're susceptible to burnout, too.

I'm not going to tell you that you can 'self-care' those feelings away or that those problems will magically disappear with time. They won't. My hope is that with more strategies in your toolkit, you'll be able to confidently identify ways to help your team and yourself – and therefore improve the work you produce. Beyond what I've mentioned so far for your direct reports, what will be helpful for you will likely be identifying a mentor, establishing boundaries (do not overwork!), learning which battles to pick, and commiserating with someone who also is currently in your position. When work gets tough, remind yourself why you do what you do.

For me, nothing is more satisfying than seeing a young person I've helped develop write something they're proud of. I'm still in touch with my mentees, all these years later, and I love hearing about what they're doing now. That's the thing about working with young people; their vision for the future is inspiring. Food media is, and will be, so much better because of them.

Un Asiento En La Mesa: Musings on Food and Cinema

Yoshivel Elise Chirinos

Food media has been a somewhat elusive pursuit for me since university. I first became aware of the career path in my teens, and I only became fascinated by it when I entered adulthood. Anthony Bourdain was my first big creative and professional inspiration. Through his television show I realised that food, culture and visual entertainment could find a home on the screen. And people responded to it, including this young Latina girl from Queens.

Of course, as plenty of curious young people do, I continued to collect a handful of other creative muses across the arts, especially in cinema. Scorsese entranced me with paper-thin slices of garlic in *Goodfellas* (1990). Eggs became strangely erotic, sliding between lovers' lips in *Tampopo* (1985). Full transparency, when I first watched a low-resolution YouTube clip of that scene at around nineteen years old, I didn't quite know what I was looking at. I've since grown to appreciate Juzo Itami's directorial decision. And of course, it'd be remiss of me to not mention *Ratatouille* (2007), which EVERYONE KNOWS is all about rats eating cheese and grapes around Paris, and Remy fiercely creating the best plate of ratatouille known to man (to rat?) while simultaneously organising a rat-centric brigade de cuisine. All of this is to say that while these films, and many more, hold a special place in my heart, I've carried this nagging feeling that something is missing for me as a cinema-lover.

When I was initially presented with the opportunity to contribute to this anthology, I was very much underemployed (some might even go as far as to say that I was in fact unemployed) and looking to break into the food media space. I first met Zoe during an uncertain time in my life (ya gotta love your twenties). I had managed to get a volunteering gig at a food and literature conference hosted by *Cherry Bombe* magazine. It had only been a week or so since that first meeting when Zoe asked me to write a piece for *Serving Up*. Over tea and toast at a cafe somewhere in the West Village of New York City, Zoe suggested that I think about what my essay would cover. What did I care about? What did I have to say? After years of academic writing and creative burnout I was unsure of what I had left to share with the world, let alone what still moved me. This was when I decided to go back to my roots and recentre myself in the interests that have driven me for most of my life thus far: food and cinema.

On the surface these topics may appear disparate, but in my brain, they have always been interconnected. I'm the kind of person that watches almost any film and is almost always more drawn to scenes of characters eating at a diner, chewing their dinner tensely at a table, or cooking an enormous feast than any other aspect of the movie. Even the frankest of conversations can be had in the most casual of settings – for example, in *When Harry Met Sally* (1989), when the titular characters at New York's famous Katz's Deli on the Lower East Side debate orgasms and female pleasure over some deli sandwiches. Sally, turkey and Harry, pastrami. A tense dinner scene that comes to mind is from Sofia Coppola's 2017 film *The Beguiled,* where all the women and girls at the table quietly, but perhaps not so subtly, vie for injured soldier John McBurney's (played by Colin Farrell) attention. The only light source in an otherwise dark room is some faint candlelight. Interestingly, the only male character meets his demise via poisonous mushrooms. (Something about what I'm going to call 'revenge fungi' or 'put guys in their place fungi' had an absolute chokehold on 2017 cinema.) And cooking an enormous spread will always make me think of the multi-course Italian feast in *Big Night* (1996). The film's a classic for a reason. We all know how epic that scene is of Stanley Tucci (playing Secondo) and Tony Shalhoub (playing Primo) plating the giant timpano. Then there's *Women on the Verge of a Nervous Breakdown* (1988). I can still hear Carmen Maura's Pepa reciting the recipe for a truly knockout (pun completely intended) gazpacho. And finally, there's my beloved *Phantom Thread* (2017).

Before anyone comes for me, yes, *Phantom Thread* is more a food film than a fashion film and I stand by that sentiment. Have y'all truly watched that first encounter between Reynolds and Alma at the hotel restaurant? The one where he, being a hungry boy, orders a hefty breakfast including lapsang souchong tea and Welsh rarebit with a poached egg? Their interaction was like a dance; a test of each other's personalities. Or how about the final scene, where Alma lovingly sautées her foraged poisonous wild mushrooms for her man. I can't help but imagine that the Spice Girls, and probably Generation Z, would affectionately regard Alma's move as 'Girl Power'. As I'm writing this, I'm beginning to see a correlation between my fascination with *Women on the Verge* and *Phantom Thread*. In *Women on the Verge*, Pepa, the protagonist, spikes her homemade gazpacho with sleeping pills in response to her nervous breakdown. In *Phantom Thread*, Alma cooks poisonous mushrooms for Reynolds Woodcock, making him violently ill. When this happens he becomes sweeter with her. In other words, during these times he values her and realises that he needs her rather than the other way around. Talk about Reynolds getting the most fungi-heavy humbling of his life. Surprisingly, he was always game for future helpings; a true glutton for punishment, if I do say so myself.

What I have come to realise about these movies, and many more that I hold near and dear to my heart, is that while they use food as an enticing storytelling vehicle, most do not feel representative of the diverse cuisines and cultures that I've been fortunate enough to experience in my life, especially as a person of colour. Rarely do I see shows or films that are reflective of Latino cultures, foods and eating traditions. Just as most people long to relate to characters and stories in the movies, so do I. There are, however, a couple of movies that come to mind when I think of food and Latino representation: *Chef* (2014) and *Beatriz at Dinner* (2017). Upon revisiting these two films recently (I hadn't watched them in years) I found that while each narrative attempts to depict Latino experiences through food and eating, one is an insightful hit and the other an underwhelming miss. Even so, *Beatriz at Dinner* and *Chef* both annoy me and inspire me as they make me think about the truths and stereotypes of Latino representation and experiences through the vehicles of food and eating. I'd encourage you to consider this as an exercise in thoughtful observation rather than a scathing critique of either film. To quote Tyra Banks, I hope that we can all 'learn something from this!' This is me using tough love to tell the film industry that when I yell like this it's because I love them.

Beatriz at Dinner

Beatriz at Dinner functions as a social commentary organised by courses: appetiser, main and dessert. The protagonist, Beatriz Luna, a holistic medicine practitioner played by Salma Hayek, is invited to dinner at a sprawling California mansion. The film makes an interesting point by depicting dinner party interactions through social and conversational etiquette. There is a sense of awkwardness when one attempts to 'fit in'. Dinner parties are great fodder for the unseen energies between people, and personally I've felt conflicted between being myself and presenting a 'palatable' version of myself to others at middle- to upper-class, white-majority dinners or cocktail functions. Firstly, there's the observation that there isn't anyone who looks like you in the space you're in, or that there are very few that do. It quickly becomes tiresome when you're wanting to get to know people over a nice glass of pinot noir and someone goes: 'Your hair is gorgeous.

Can I touch it?' and then before I can say no, I'm being petted like I'm a Havanese. Suddenly I feel like everyone's eyes are on me, in a manner that I don't particularly care for, and my glass of wine has gone rancid.

In one scene Beatriz is asked an insensitive question that many people of colour have encountered once, or countless times, before: 'Where are you from? Where are you REALLY from?' Beatriz answers that she is originally from a Mexican town near the Pacific. Another dinner guest says, 'Mexico's awesome. I love Cancun.' As a viewer I could not help but laugh at the Cancun comment. It serves as a superficial contribution to the conversation but also highlights how some people try to communicate an understanding or interest in another's culture by mentioning an innocuous fact or anecdote. If I had a dime for every time I've mentioned in a conversation that I am half-Puerto Rican and half-Honduran and someone has immediately asked if I'm 'spicy' or if I use the same lipstick as AOC, then I'd have enough dough to pay off my student loans. To address the latter: yes, I do use the same lipstick as Ms Alexandria Ocasio-Cortez. It's Stila's Stay All Day Liquid Lipstick in 'Beso' and it's fabulous. But that's beside the point.

I once attended a press lunch where all the guests had beautiful handwritten place cards. A personalised place card was a first for me and I was so excited to take a picture of it to memorialise on Instagram. I mean if you didn't take a pic, were you ever really there? When it was time to take our seats at this long charmingly decorated table, I looked down at my place card, and that's when I saw that my name was misspelled. And of course, Harry and Sally's and so on weren't. I knew that it was a privilege for me to sit down and break bread with the carefully curated guest-list that I found myself seated with. It was disappointing, however, to see everyone else gush over their seating cards and take photos except me. I covered my card with a napkin and proceeded with mingling. Mingling in these situations usually leads to the mention of how 'strange' or 'unique' my name is. 'Where is it from?', 'What's your background?', 'Oh, you're Honduran? I went on vacation there once,' and finally, 'I love SPANISH food but there's too much spice.'

In the film, Beatriz regains control of the conversation by posing the same question back to Doug, the rich white host: 'Where are you from? But where are you REALLY from?' Since this question is rarely asked of someone who is white-American, he is caught off guard. Doug reacts defensively by asking Beatriz about her professional training, her education, and finally her immigration status. She replies that she came to the United States legally when Doug retorts: 'And how'd that work?', inappropriately calling her immigration status into question. I had to pause the film at that point because it makes my blood boil; it stirs an anger in me that should arouse the same reaction in anyone who has even an ounce of self-awareness. I see my neighbours and my relatives in that interaction and it cements how common microaggressions like these are. When the final dinner guests arrive and talk in the foyer, Beatriz hangs back and watches from the opposite side of the room, slowly savouring her glass of white wine. Everyone walks past Beatriz as if she does not exist, but she follows the group from behind. At moments when I would typically introduce my guest to other party-goers, I too have often been left at the doorway to introduce myself and attempt to mingle on my own.

The film sets up Beatriz to be an observer; an outsider looking in. It's a perspective that I am familiar with. It's that feeling of being on the periphery, wanting to hold a meaningful conversation with someone but being met with rigidity because as hard as you try, they can't quite empathise with your truth. Beatriz enters the kitchen in Doug's Californian mansion where she finds a personal chef and a house manager named Evan, played by John Early, silently preparing vegetables for dinner. There's a colourful array of produce on the kitchen island; it is the only vibrancy to be found during our tour of the otherwise cold, museum-like home. Only the chef visibly acknowledges Beatriz and greets her. Here, I am reminded of Anthony Bourdain's comment about the bones of the American restaurant industry relying heavily on Latino-immigrant workers.[1] The porters, the kitchen staff, the dishwashers. We're everywhere. And from an even more personal standpoint it makes me think of some of my aunts and cousins, acquaintances and neighbours who work as night cleaners, bathroom attendants, house cleaners. I was raised to thank workers for what they contribute. So if I see a bus boy or a dishwasher after or during a meal I acknowledge them. I say thank you. Same when I see a cleaner enter the office as I'm clocking out for the night. I see them. And in a way I know them. I know what they contribute. Saying thanks is the very least that I, or for that matter anyone else, can do.

Chef

In comparison, a better-known 'food movie' from a few years earlier, *Chef*, is a light-hearted film that either intentionally or unintentionally emphasises Latino stereotypes and white-saviour inclinations. *Chef* introduces the protagonist Carl (played by Jon Favreau) and Martin (played by John Leguizamo) and right off the bat we have casting choices that illustrate a particular image of power. Martin, the person of colour, is a line cook, while his senior chef de cuisine is a white man who gets all the acclaim and attention for the food at the restaurant they're employed at. Martin is first seen hauling a giant pig carcass over his shoulders and essentially doing the dirty work while Carl painstakingly butchers the meat. I read this scene as Carl being portrayed as the competent, refined artistic force in the kitchen while Martin serves as loyal sidekick to him. As the film progresses this dynamic continues, and in addition Martin and his Latino identity are also used for comic relief.

Almost every time Martin is in a scene his Latinidad is used for laughs. In one scene Martin takes out a tray of disappointingly overcooked bacon. He exclaims, 'When I find out who it is, grab your ankles, 'cause here comes Papi Chulo.' Food film or not, I find that when a film has a Latino character, they'll emphasise their otherness by throwing in Spanglish dialogue or slang. It's as if a character cannot exist in the world of the film without demonstrating their background. This happens multiple times throughout *Chef*. Strangely, it also portrays Carl as the expert in Latin flavours and Cuban cuisine, which cements the white man's position of power. Carl takes it upon himself to 'enlighten' others about Cuban food and he uses this to professionally pivot from being the head chef of a chic, reputable Los Angeles restaurant to trying his luck as the owner of a food truck where he can call the creative shots.

In another scene, Martin tastes some new dishes that Carl is testing out. Martin asks, 'What's that?' Carl replies, 'It's carne asada.' I found this short dialogue inauthentic, because if Martin is written to be a 'truly' Latino character who has worked in kitchens for many years, then he would certainly be able to recognise carne asada. Yet Carl is the one who clarifies what it is, emphasising him as the expert. It isn't until Martin is at Carl's food truck later in the film when we finally see him cook and show his culinary prowess. He makes mojo, and prepares and cooks the pernil for the Cuban sandwiches. But Carl continues to be portrayed as THE authority on Cuban cuisine. In a scene at a restaurant-equipment store, he teaches his son Percy about what a plancha is and how it is used to make Cuban sandwiches. Carl is also the one who teaches his son how to assemble a Cuban sandwich. In another scene, Carl teaches his son about yucca and plátanos as they shop for fresh ingredients. When Carl quits his position as chef de cuisine it leaves Martin and the rest of the staff to contend with a full house. What we see next is a montage of the team floundering as they try to keep up with piling orders. The idea that scene communicates is that the chef's brigade, made up largely of people of colour, are almost helpless without him. And when the employees choose to stay at the restaurant and not walk out with him, they are choosing the stuffiness of haute French cuisine over artistic expression. It is Carl that has the clarity of heart and mind to see non-European cuisine as legitimate and worth pursuing, but actually it's the chef's brigade who are really choosing, or prioritising, stability and secure employment over joining Carl's risky business pursuits.

Following a public meltdown, which is filmed and shared on the internet, Carl is left jobless, and he, his ex-wife Inez, played by Sofia Vergara, and Percy take a trip to Miami. On their first night there they eat at the iconic Cuban restaurant Versailles. I will say that I was ecstatic to see this gastronomic institution acknowledged in a movie. The joy on everyone's faces while eating their yucca and sandwiches appeared genuine. Of course, this glimmer of realistic representation subsides. When Carl finally secures a food truck, Martin asks him what he is planning to cook. 'Cuban sandwiches, plátanos, arroz con pollo. Simple shit like we used to do for family meals.' Forgive me if this brings me back to my childhood when I proudly brought in my mother's budin de pan for my classmates to try. I remember someone picking at it and asking, 'What's that?' and commenting that it looked 'like cat food'. I never saw my food that way and I was petrified when I heard those words. That same 'cat food' is now lusted after on TikTok. And just like the self-proclaimed food experts on TikTok, it's Carl who's presented as the 'cultured culinary saviour'. He is the one who truly sees the value of 'simple' cooking and selling Cuban food, and it's somehow his job to spread the gospel to others as well. When Carl needs help loading new kitchen appliances into the truck, in Spanish Martin offers some nearby workers an amazing sandwich by 'the best chef in the world' if they help. If they decline Martin threatens to call immigration. Although this was a fleeting scene, this interaction frustrated me. I felt that it painted a Latino person to be insensitive to the issues facing his community, whereas Carl was spared the job of threatening the workers to uphold the role of the 'good cop'.

Digestif

Taking the time to rewatch both *Beatriz at Dinner* and *Chef* reminded me of the small steps that have been made to portray the intricacies of the Latino experience in cinema. I am critical of these works because I believe that the 'seventh art' is capable of achieving so much more nuance than it currently does. There is still a huge amount of work that needs to be done to accurately present the diversity of our experiences on the screen. Latinos are far from one dimensional; we are complex people who balance both shared and unique identities. Food and the act of eating can be a vehicle for, or an insightful way of, presenting nuances of cultural heritage through a visual medium. In order to achieve this, proper research and experts who identify with these experiences must be included in the production process. This is a tactful way of me saying: 'Hollywood, hire me and others like me YESTERDAY,' because we've been INCREDIBLY PATIENT in waiting to see ourselves behind, and in front of, the camera. In the meantime, I'll continue to write screenplays in my bedroom, spark conversations on food and representation in cinema, and one day soon make my own film.

'It's too spicy' and Other Such Bullshit

Fatima 'Fatti' Tarkleman

Sitting unwashed and depressed in just my pants on the sofa, eating my listless toast dinner, and watching a well-known TV cooking competition that pits established UK chefs against each other. An amazing Welsh-Thai chef, whose food I had been lucky enough to try, is in the firing line. One judge after another delivers the same infuriating feedback: 'It's too spicy.' One judge comments, 'It's numbing my palate so I can't taste anything.' Another moans, 'Your problem here is the chilli.'

I was enraged, shouting fuck off, toast crumbs flying out of my mouth, watching a bunch of predominantly white chefs invalidate the chef's food. When my partner and I ate his powerfully flavourful, dainty take on a Thai jungle curry we commented on how refreshing it was that we could actually feel the dish's chilli heat. This rage is more than just an annoyance at how wrong the judges are. It is as if they are talking to me, dictating what flavours are 'acceptable', defining the 'standards', and rubbing a fistful of chilli-spiked salt into a wound that I had only just discovered.

That wound may have been festering for some time, though, and my journey to this crumb-covered sofa may help identify why it hurt so much.

Prior to becoming a chef, I worked for a decade in the NHS as an occupational therapist. The NHS's culture is infamously exhausting, but it did impress upon me how it was possible – and very important – to be kind and respectful, even when working under high-stress conditions. Despite loving most of it, years of being in a woefully under-resourced sector slowly chipped away at my mental health. I burned out and I was depressed. I absorbed all the dysfunctional bureaucracy and tragedy that I observed, had too many panic attacks, and knew I had to move on. I did what any respectable adult does when faced with important career choices: RUN AWAY! I spent fifteen months exploring a world of flavours: crunchy kachori in India, Cambodian amok, khao soi in the hills of Northern Thailand, grilled fish with sour mango in night markets of Borneo, feijoada of Río, Argentinian helados, Salento's limonada de coco, tamales on Lake Atitlán, lime-chilli crickets, crayfish, sushi, and then eventually went back home to dream about all that wild deliciousness.

I was well fed, buzzing from the realisation that food brought me comfort during my uncertainty. I watched weeks of cooking TV and fantasised longingly about working in a restaurant kitchen. I impulse-bought cookbooks I couldn't afford and started working my way through them.

'IT'S TOO SPICY' AND OTHER SUCH BULLSHIT

Sometimes I wasn't even eating the food (depression can make caring about eating difficult) but after some months of heavy drinking, meditative salty fry-ups and warm encouragement from friends, I decided to become a chef. Food brings me the purest pleasure. It was at the heart of the events I went to, the media I consumed, how others cared for me and how I nourished the ones I love. Food connects me to family, friends and community. Plus, being praised for making a great meal also fed my depleted ego, so fuck it, I said: I am going be the best damn chef I can be, chef. YES, CHEF!

I blagged a job in a cafe and then somehow entered the oxymoronic world of casual fine dining. It was like a beautiful, chaotic dream. The food was so damn good and I was inspired by every morsel. I was living my chef fantasy, but gradually began to notice uglier aspects of the kitchen's culture. I was laughed at for requesting a break during a very illegal sixteen-hour shift. I was mocked for needing a stool to reach the high-shelf ingredients. There were too many Irish and gay jokes. Kitchen porters were belittled. Chef 'banter' normalised stories of bullying and abuse, and colleagues frequently boasted about how little sleep they'd had. The strict hierarchy and blame culture was oppressive and my NHS training quickly identified the ticking time bomb of mental health problems that surrounded me. I also noticed that Eurocentric foods and techniques were casually referred to as superior to others, with anything else treated as 'unrefined comfort food'.

Three months later I moved on to a gastropub in southeast London where everyone was kinder to each other, the food was fantastic and I was inspired all over again. That said, apart from one scotch bonnet item on the menu, it was clear that little effort was put into making the restaurant accessible to the local community, a high proportion of whom were people of colour. It was uncomfortable to walk into the sea of white faces sitting at the tables, while so many black and brown faces were walking around outside. I had swapped an inaccessible kitchen for an inaccessible menu. The food was not for the locals and, to me, the restaurant's existence felt like an unsavoury step towards gentrification. A few months later, a change in medication made my anxiety sink through the floor and my sick leave was handled spectacularly poorly by my boss. I had to bring umpteen GP letters to prove that I wasn't skiving. My chef dream was quickly turning pretty hellish.

I looked up around me, dazed and disheartened at all the glaring red flags and questions. Chefs are disposable, and if you don't like your Victorian-era workplace conditions, then you can be sacked that day with little consequence. Why are you expected to work double shifts, no matter how that impacts on your own life, when the links between sleep and mental health are so well documented? Why is the fact that four out of five chefs in the country experience severe work-related mental health difficulties not considered an industry crisis?[1] Why is the prevalence of addiction in hospitality so widely overlooked? Why is everyone who isn't a manager so undervalued and treated like a brainless worker-drone? Where are all the people of colour in senior positions in the industry? And who the actual fuck has the right to say that fiery, spicy chilli heat, enjoyed by swathes of nations, is too much?

There had to be a better way than the dysfunctional

systems I'd observed. I still wanted to be a chef, and now I also wanted to champion those of us from marginalised communities. Then, like a tiny little miracle, my lovely buddy Kaajal Modi hired me to be a chef in her arts PhD project. We started a project called Kitchen Cultures in which care was central, and women of colour were given the spotlight to express their heritage through food. The opportunity reshaped my practice, and over the past two years I have been building a collaborative cookbook, *Kin-spiration*, that prioritises the recipes of womxn and non-binary chefs of colour. It is a piece of soft activism; an opportunity for us to take a small step towards redressing the inequity in the industry. I started an Instagram page as a kind of online CV, and followed amazing women and non-binary chefs of colour, and took note of those who, like myself, wanted to change hospitality into a less toxic, more diverse environment to work in. More recently, I founded the queer dating supperclub, Eat Cute, where single and polyamorous people (like myself) can meet and eat in safer surroundings. We are an all-queer team. I have found employment with people doing the good work from the ground up – managing their workplaces in a way to empower marginalised groups.

It was hugely validating to know that there are others out there like me, who weren't afraid to point out the glaring inequalities and health risks in the industry and shape their businesses to do better, value their staff, and be kind about it. All these amazing people became my online hospitality community and helped me get through a terrifying and exceptionally stressful year. The current, toxic standards allow the industry to tolerate dubious employment practices and foster abusive and inaccessible workplaces, which sees marginalised groups having to do a lot more to gain access to parts of the industry dominated by their cis-het white male counterparts. As a queer migrant of colour, I exist on many intersections and want to see marginalised groups experience less prejudice to be able to thrive in this industry. I want those of you who eat out at restaurants with glossy exteriors to consider not just what the restaurant says they stand for, but what they are actively doing to redress these glaring inequalities in their ethically murky kitchens. 'It's too spicy' is so painful to hear because it is telling me that what I want is unacceptable. It is a damaging attack on cultural diversity and highlights the dangerous reluctance of a foodie scene to look beyond its elitist, bigoted rigidity.

I have turned off the TV and dusted off the crumbs to go and join the chef community that I have found. We are bringing new flavours to this industry's oppressive menu. It's not too spicy.

In fact, it's not spicy enough.

The Things We Could Not Swallow: On 'Good' Taste, Identity and Grief

Cynthia Greenlee

I ate the lemongrass soppressata with a question mark on my palate (lemongrass and soppressata?). The dried salami came with tangy dipping sauces and a free serving of self-loathing.

Charcuterie boards entice the petit bourgeoisie. I fully include myself among that number. Circa 2022, these ostentatious and often expensive snack slabs are big business for white women who were, only a few years back, hawking cupcakes. The domestic-doyenne who can artfully arrange gentrified vegetables and carve crude blossoms can get what she wants with comestible crafts.

I didn't want to admit that my charcuterie splurge was a failed experiment in fusion. But sitting at a sleek gastropub and picking at the assorted meat, I longed for a basket from the local mall's Hickory Farms holiday pop-up. At least I could count on the summer sausage, outrageously orange American Cheddar and strawberry bonbons for satisfaction.

My father would have pointed out the folly of these luxe cold cuts. He probably would have taken one sausage round and, talking with mouth full, asked me how much I spent on this tray. Without thinking, I'd tell him half the price and hope that was cheap enough to end the conversation. For who would pay $40 for about a dozen quarter-sized rounds of cured meat, a sprinkle of nuts, glorified Wheat Thins, picayune cheese wedges, a spot of jam, a daub of truffle paste and vinegary pickled okra?

He would have been just as pleased – more pleased – with a hot dog. And to speak the honest-to-God truth, so would I.

When dementia took my father's ability to swallow right out of his throat, the nursing-home staff explicitly banned hot dogs unless they were diced into minuscule, flesh-coloured squares. *He could choke*, they said. I saw the wisdom of this restriction. But I wondered how long my father could survive without his favourite treat. What was life without the tactile joy of holding a hot dog in hand and biting into it, feeling that casing pop-snap?

Miserably staring at the tiny stacks of cured meat, I thought, *What I wouldn't give to have a hot dog with my father again.*

The Common Man's Charcuterie

Under my father's watchful eye, I had consumed many a gas-station hot dog as a child. He'd pump the gas, then walk inside to pay the tab, and grab a hot dog, or nabs, packaged cheesy crackers that made perfect travelling snacks.

Wilco, a gas station on Summit Avenue a few miles from our ranch house in Greensboro, North Carolina, was our favourite pit stop. Hot dogs glistened and rolled in that small oven, with varying degrees of freshness. Even if the hot dog was wrinkled like fingers soaked too long in the bath, I knew that we could dependably find this meal in a bun there. Even my mother – who experimented with quiche, clam dip and fried rice in our house, and took me to Vietnamese restaurants and mansion teahouses – could be persuaded to have what she called a 'dirty hot dog'. Rare was the time that I couldn't convince my father to spend a buck for a hot dog. This was not my accomplishment, but a statement of how much he loved a hot dog 'all the way' Carolina style: chilli (no beans), relish, mustard squiggle, raw white onion, ketchup, slaw. The hot dog itself doesn't matter much – pork or beef, thin or plumped – but the bun should be slightly soggy. This is one time when mushiness is a virtue.

If I have a realpolitik of food, it includes a love affair with hidden or stigmatised kitchens, the ones where the food comes wrapped in foil, and that food is more likely to be artificial and mass-produced than artisanal. Judge me if you will. Gas-station hot dogs made me the egalitarian eater that I am, who can go for haute cuisine or humble meals. I understand that there is no more worth in a white tablecloth than a greasy truck-stop bag. Restaurants are not the only venue where we meet food and ourselves.

I cherished Saturday outings with my father, a veteran and social worker who could at times be a severe disciplinarian.

Forget to take out the trash, and he'd subtract a quarter from my $2-a-week allowance; I learned negative numbers early, in second grade, because my lax commitment to chores dropped me into deficits again and again.

But on some weekends, when he shed his business clothes for coarse Wrangler jeans and a polo shirt, I'd go with him to wondrous places like the feed store FCX, the Farmers Cooperative Exchange. It smelled tinny like fertiliser, green like seedlings, and sugary from taffy knots in giant barrels. It was a marvellous mélange.

I can tell you the story of my relationship with my father through processed meats. If it were lunchtime when we left the feed store, we'd venture to Mr Dunderbak's in the mall, a chain deli and market that was like a German-themed Hickory Farms. Every day there was mock-Oktoberfest. He'd order wurst, a stein of beer, and I'd swing my legs from atop a barstool. We'd order a pound of German bologna from the case stuffed with giant tubes of meat, an offering to my mother, one meal she wouldn't have to cook herself.

We most often ate at home on our table crammed into the kitchen, from a predictable menu, for my father was adamant about what he would eat and what he would not. Meals had to have a meat, vegetables and a bread. That meat most often chosen was Salisbury steak, or fried or oven-baked chicken. No pasta, no shrimp, no Chinese food. When our father capitulated and finally tried pizza – and when Domino's finally bucked redlining to tiptoe carefully into our Black neighbourhood – it was a miracle. Our mother, though, tried her hand at everything: oyster dip in the 1960s, Texas sheet cake in the 1970s, quiches in the 1980s, beer-chicken standing upright in the 1990s oven. She introduced me to Shanghai noodles and escorted me in a fancy dress to full tea.

When she dies, she told me her funeral repast has to be just so: no fried chicken, for who would make her signature dish better than she? She would not abide terrible chicken – or be upstaged – at her Last Supper. Roast chicken and salmon, because choice is good in life as it is in death. Macaroni with a saltine crust. Bok choy as the green. Or if we must have green beans, they must not be in those giant gallon cans, but hand-snapped and blanched.

Sometimes I'm feeling bok choy. Other days, I'm into those store-brand green beans. Sometimes, it's charcuterie for me. Sometimes, many times, it is hot dogs.

But sometimes, many times, there seems to be no divide between the upper-crust food and ultra-processed eats. After all, what is pâté but liver mush with a French accent? Most days, if we are what we eat, I'm both charcuterie and hot dogs, definitely Carolina style.

There are people with whom you eat, and then there are people who teach you how to eat. I know I'm my father's daughter because at a family cookout, where an aunt pushed us 'philistines' to abandon hot dogs for salmon, the choice was clear to me. As it was to the rest of the kinfolk who didn't agree with our relative, who had a reputation for trying to be big-time and disparaging others. The fish languished. The hog dog pile diminished with astonishing speed. Though my family has pretentions aplenty, those affectations don't extend to the edible composite that is the hot dog. And no one goes to a cookout for omega-3 fatty acids.

The Partisan of Processed Meats

My father's name was Ralph, and my mother often pronounced it like 'Rolfe', as if he were some prince of the crumbling Habsburg Empire. I secretly called him the Bishop of Baloney.

He was a child of the Depression and a family that had a bumper crop of children. Meat had to stretch far and wide. He sometimes made fun of my mother's South Carolina family for being country. My mother once retorted, *At least we had meat.* Meat from freshly slaughtered cows, hams curing in the smokehouse. It was one of the few times I saw the proverbial cat snatch my dad's tongue. I understand how much-maligned baloney was both a convenience food and a luxury item for him growing up: low cost but a respite from the yardbird and other meat you had to shoot, strangle or otherwise kill for dinner.

I inherited his unspoken quest for the perfect hot dog, and it took me to places. Certainly not the grand tour of Europe, though I've eaten street dogs in *calles* and alleys worldwide. To the hidey holes where people eat, where menus don't exist, where sweaty men in work clothes eat in the sun, where we drink Coke out the bottle and do the uncouth thing of drinking without a straw (I've never aspired to be a lady). When my father picked me up from college on some weekends, we'd stop at Zack's (an iconic restaurant in Graham, North Carolina) where the waiters served hot dogs – what else? – and carried them lined up along on their inner arms.

On my frequent visits home, I'd fall back into my childhood routine. I had become, belatedly, an only child at age thirteen. My older sisters, who were fourteen months apart, departed to college at roughly the same time. I was the last of the children to rear and as the youngest in my immediate family (and the youngest grandchild in my generation), I was called upon to perform random tasks. Someone had to do the running until someone among us created another generation of tiny labourers, indentured to our elders.

More nights than not, my father called my name in the interregnum between dinner and bedtime. He called on me more than Jesus. He'd ask for a bologna sandwich, repeating the same directions, as if I hadn't heard them for years: one slice of white bread, Oscar Mayer thick bologna, the slightest sheen of mayonnaise, occasionally a tangy mustard smear. And a glass of milk.

The bologna's pinkness grossed me out. I'd gag, seeing half-moons of composite meat under my fingertips after I peeled the red sticky tape from its edges. But I stifled my gag reflex and learned to deliver him comfort with cold cuts.

The Mourning Menu

It's the first week of lockdown during the pandemic. My mother calls and tells me, 'You need to come.' I know she is saying that my father is dying without saying my father is dying. It is a shock but not a shock. We have not been able to talk to him, really talk to him, since the nursing home closed. No family is allowed. We can't talk on the phone because he can't figure out which way to hold the receiver. And without the daily interactions with his friends in the dining hall, without the open doors through which hallmates wave and he can see the world, he loses his words quickly.

I am eating bad nursing-home chow mein as my father lies dying, his fingernails turning bluer by the minute. They send meals, free of charge, from the cafeteria when someone is dying. I start to have some reaction, my face burning and my cheekbones swelling to make my eyes small and pig-like. As his body turns off the lights, my immune system is throwing an unwanted and troublesome surprise party.

'MSG,' says my mother matter-of-factly. And I start to remind her that MSG isn't the danger it was made out to be. I revert to the rational. And then I remember my father is dying. She gives me a Benadryl. I smooth lotion over my face, wondering if someone has an EpiPen and if we will be burying two family members for the price of one. I want to go with him, wherever his final destination is.

We are the first family to have a funeral in this small mountain town during lockdown. Only five people can be in the receiving room with my father's body. My mother, sisters and I make four. We take turns so cousins and aunts can say goodbye. We make it through the Zoom funeral without a flicker of the WiFi. And we go home because there is no repast. We cannot gather to fete my father's life with a meal prepared by a loving assembly line of church ladies. They have staffed every funeral service with helpings of green beans, mac and cheese, chicken and pound cake. But most of them – many my aunts and cousins – are dead, and no one wants a funeral to be a superspreading event. Covid robbed us of ritual.

The next day, Middle Sister and I sit outside at a local butcher shop. We order gourmet hot dogs from the window. Our father wouldn't abide us paying $8 a pop for a hot dog, and they don't even have chilli. The owners must be Northerners, we reason. Clearly, they don't know any better.

Door-dash Repast

I struggled to write this essay for two, almost three years. Four years without my father. Even now, I'm doubtful it is coherent. You decide, though understand I am not writing it for you.

This essay began as a love letter to the man who made me appreciate humble food, but it refused all efforts at editorial taming.

Grief is unwieldy,
    obdurate, cares nothing for your deadlines,
        says 'I prefer not to' like Bartleby the Scrivener.

Perhaps I am writing in circles to avoid a repeat of the wild suffering that consumed me in the immediate aftermath of my father's death. I've learned that I'm the person who screams at funerals, unable to control my hiccup-sobs that soon turn into howls. My hair fell out in great chunks within twenty-four hours of his passing. My dog's death, days after his, prompted a grocery store panic attack; I couldn't stop heaving though I knew police might be on their way. I didn't want to compound my mother's sorrow by becoming another Black person whose mental health crisis became reason for murder. I couldn't eat three meals a day for months. I couldn't pass my father's favourite breakfast joint without holding my breath.

Of all the things I couldn't do, I couldn't write my way through it. And what use are you, as a writer, if you can't suture your own wounds with words, time and food?

On the second anniversary of my father's death, my mother

is content to spend the day in quiet contemplation. But I'm itching to do something, uncomfortable with the fact that after all this time, we haven't been able to give my father the last supper that was his due, to gather with those who love him.

I leave the house and drive to the grocery story. I drop about $100 on food containers, packs of hot dogs and buns, canned chilli, tubs of creamy slaw, jars of relish.

I carefully assemble do-it-yourself Carolina hot dog kits for family. 'A special delivery from Daddy,' I say when I ring relatives' doorbells and give them the containers. I can't take their emotions and quickly, awkwardly hightail it to my car.

Say what you will – that heaven isn't real. Or that manna and ambrosia dominate celestial menus, not offerings so carnal and mundane as a processed meat.

I'm not sure if I believe in the Great Ever-After, but if it exists, afterlife chow is whatever you want it to be. Heaven could be the bar that never cuts you off, handing out free and eternal Tequila Sunrises while Tupac shit-talks in a vinyl booth that never cracks, slow-sipping peppermint schnapps with Jackie Wilson and Sam Cooke. Or an endless supply of pancakes on a Sunday morning; a legendary brunch spot.

Say what you will – that hot dogs are cow lips compressed with the nastiest of the nasty, nitratey bits. Say, as a recent study did, that every time you eat a hot dog, thirty-six hours fall off your already-brief life, and that life is far too precious to give up more of it for a workaday weiner.[1] But still I hope, for him and for me, that heaven is lined with hot dogs.

Eating Our Feelings: The Role of Food in Death Rituals, and How It Helps Us Process Loss

Tiffani Rozier

One memory that truly stands out to me about my grandmother is her love for anything crispy and crackling. She had a particular fondness for the ultra-crunchy texture found in the red box of Banquet's frozen fried chicken – although the actual meat content was often overwhelmed by batter or breading. But that didn't stop her from relishing every morsel, leaving no chicken bone untouched.

It's been fourteen years since Johnnie Ruth transitioned, and I welcome the familiar things that keep me tethered to her light. At the risk of sounding hyperbolic, I'm convinced that she was one of the most brilliant minds of the twentieth century. She had a deep love and affection for Arizona and the Southwest. She spent most of her adulthood making her way back there. Whenever I stumble upon a bag of pork rinds or a box of orange pekoe tea in a grocery store, I am transported back to the warmth of her Phoenix apartment, the sound of her pencil scratching out answers on one of her many crossword puzzles, and the smell of newsprint and hot black tea. She would tear the crossword out of random newspapers and store them in a wicker basket tucked next to her worn-out, beige recliner, waiting for her to apply her brilliance.

I lived with her for some time in my twenties. Around my grandmother, I felt seen, heard and understood. I slept on her scratchy, vintage couch and watched her be exasperated at the contestants on *Jeopardy*, cackle at reruns of *Bonanza*, and become wholeheartedly invested in every episode of *Star Trek: The Next Generation*. She was a sharp woman, an educator – she did not suffer fools. She had an insatiable curiosity, a core value that I inherited. I also inherited her sense of humour, facial commentary, and passion for writing and storytelling.

Experiencing the physical loss of someone you love is abrupt and feels violent. Against that violence, food is a shield. The moments I regret most are the meals my grandmother and I didn't get to share. Those missed meals feel like missed conversations and connections. That feeling of regret is why I think food plays such a central role in the grieving process. Food is a gift, a statement of care. It says, 'I cherish you and the memories we made together.'

Her knack for making fry bread and biscuits is something I will forever be curious about. I've harboured a suspicion that it is somehow connected to the family legend that her mother, my great-grandmother, was a young Hopi woman. The Hopi nation is the westernmost group of Pueblo

Indians, occupying what is now north-eastern Arizona. Fry bread, a traditional Native American dish, has its origins in the painful history of Native displacement. It was created out of necessity when tribes were provided government rations that included flour, sugar and lard. Despite its humble beginnings, fry bread has become a symbol of resilience and cultural pride. Though my grandmother's ancestral roots remained a mystery to her until she died I think she found a bit of solace in making fry bread. It saddens me to think that she never had the opportunity to relish her mother's warm embrace and delicious cooking. Years before my grandmother's death, the aunt that raised her passed away and left a small box that had accompanied my grandmother when she was a child. The box contained a photo of her mother among other things. It is the only one to exist, the sole image that my grandmother had of her.

Throughout history and across cultures, food has been a way to honour the departed, connect with our ancestors and soothe the pain of loss. The act of preparing and sharing food during times of grief serves as a tangible expression of love and remembrance. In many cultures, it is customary to prepare special dishes or offerings to commemorate the deceased. In my grandmother's case, the connection to her possible Hopi heritage was found when she made fry bread.

After I moved out of my grandmother's apartment, I'd visit and check her refrigerator and her pantry to make sure she was eating well. Watching her cook was an experience. I remember the knife in her kitchen. She had a knife block, and there was never anything in it. This knife sat on her counter, and it was the only one she would ever use to prepare a meal. It was a paring knife with a wooden handle. The blade was no more than half an inch long. She had used it so much that the little knife barely held an edge, and it didn't have a tip, but she did everything with it. She'd cut meat, slice bread and peel apples (in one unbroken strip). She also had a little pig-shaped, wooden cutting board. And those two things – the knife and the cutting board – would live together on her counter next to the knife block with no knives in it.

Johnnie Ruth was her own brand of grandmother. She lived for herself, unapologetically. She wasn't 'doting', she preferred solitude, she hated talking on the phone, and she never had food ready just awaiting your visit. She never called herself a cook, but she would feed you; just don't expect all that 'Big Momma' energy to be a part of the experience. She had a dish called stuffmajig (I never confirmed the spelling). It was a dish she fed my mom and her siblings when they were children. She was a Black woman raising children on her own in the 1950s and 1960s. She worked two or three jobs while completing the coursework for her degree. There were times when the cupboards were bare. Not to be defeated, my grandmother would come home and pull together all the leftovers and whatever was in the pantry, put it all in a pot, and let it do its own thing. The broken grains of rice cooked until the grain split, which gave it a beautiful texture that always reminded me of buckwheat or 닭죽 (dakjuk), Korean rice porridge. So much of her lived experience was broken, much like that rice, and she would split herself to be of service to the world and her family. And like that dish, that brokenness produced something entirely new and nourishing. It is her in a bowl, it is always delicious. I think my grandmother's stuffmajig is soul food.

My definition of soul food is that which fills your belly and feeds your soul. It may not be a pot of braised greens, cornbread, or baked macaroni and cheese, but it was a way for her heart to be in communion with ours.

In the end, food is not just sustenance for the body; it's sustenance for the soul. It carries the power to transcend time and space, connecting us with our ancestors, our memories and our deepest emotions.

As I reflect on the profound role of food in our lives, I am drawn to a poignant absence – the absence of food rituals in my family's history. This absence became starkly evident during my grandmother's funeral, where I found myself wondering why our family didn't adhere to the customary food-related rituals that seemed to be intrinsic to many other cultures and families.

It was in that moment of loss and mourning, surrounded by grieving family members, that I realised the glaring void in our traditions. Other communities had these rituals, these comforting customs that offered solace and connection during times of grief. But in my family, they were conspicuously absent.

This realisation led to a cascade of questions. Why did my family not have these rituals? Was it a matter of history, class, or perhaps even rooted in racial disparities? What was lacking that denied us the privilege of partaking in these shared experiences that other communities seemed to have so readily? As I contemplated this absence, I couldn't help but think of what it meant for the memory of my grandmother.

As more of my own birthdays pass I contemplate my own mortality. I wonder if there will be food at my funeral, and if so, what food it may be. Will someone offer my favourite chocolates or pour out my favourite bourbon on an ancestral altar?

My life has taught me that there is rarely value in seeking definitive conclusions to grand questions such as this. On my quest for understanding how food impacts memory and grief, I have found that the thrill lies in the unanswered questions, because those questions encourage me to consider how I want to be remembered and celebrated.

The last conversation I had with my grandmother was on the telephone. She was in the hospital and I was in Nashville. She called to scold me because I wasn't there to make sure her DNR was honoured. Our conversation was that of two friends with a large age gap. I asked her if she wanted me to return for her funeral and she responded, 'Absolutely not!' She told me to go live my life, because that was more important than seeing her off. Finally she said, 'Go have an ice cream cone and don't wait until you're seventy years old to have a good friend.'

My grandmother used to send me a birthday card every year with about $5 in it, and there was always a small note in her beautiful handwriting that said, 'Happy Birthday, go have an ice cream cone on me.'

Inheritance

Apoorva Sripathi

Certain things are inherited. My mother, who is from a small village in Tirunelveli in Tamil Nadu, gave me an inheritance of Chennai summer, and the rituals of preservation.

There are other legacies and rituals that I inherited as well – learning how to package stuff fastidiously, to assemble steel shelves and put together a bicycle, and to make buttermilk rasam; an old gold ring with fake gemstones that my grandfather wore as a young man, my father's collection of crime novels, my mother's tattered diaries filled with recipes, my paternal grandmother's gorgeous mango yellow silk sari, and perhaps an appetite for sour foods. But nothing has prepared me for life like preservation has. No other food ritual has given me more memories of my mother either.

As early as seven, I learned how to dry mango and pack salted lime for pickles; soak chillies and turkey berries in buttermilk and later dry them under the sun; and to reuse cooked rice in various forms from kanji to dried cooked rice balls, which she would fry in hot oil to accompany . . . rice. Every summer morning, I would drowsily accompany my mother to our terrace, armed with bundles of my father's old lungis or my grandfather's old veshtis and a long plastic sheet so I could watch her pour koozh vadam, aka rice gruel, into odd shapes. Sometimes she'd do versions with sago pearls or onions, but rice was a constant. And they'd all be flavoured with cumin, asafoetida, chilli, carom seeds – ingredients to ensure digestion – pressed into different shapes, dried in the sun for three days, and stored in tight jars only to be fried later.

It took me a while to realise that this was not only an exercise in preservation of food – making sure that we could tide over monsoon with a crispy snack or use as an emergency stash when we couldn't afford vegetables – but a preservation of time as well. This extended to vegetables, from okra and aubergine to cluster beans and black nightshade berries, all soaked in an abundance of tart buttermilk first. Buttermilk and yoghurt themselves are gifts in preservation – my mother told me that when we moved from our first address in the city to our current one, she packed a small container with a spoonful of curd to reactivate the culture in the new house. Running out of curd was a specific kind of panic my mother and my grandmother hoped to avoid all their lives. Fermentation is preservation of the present to ensure that inheritance is a possibility in the future.

Growing up, I remember feeling quite smug about this

secret preservation technique, until I looked outside my window one day to see fish and prawns being dried on my neighbour's rooftop. The second time I spotted salted, dried fish was when I travelled to my mother's old workplace, to what I once considered the edge of my city when in fact it was where the first settlement of Chennai (or Madras, as it was known then) began, in the late 1600s. Walking around George Town – christened in honour of the then Emperor of India, George V – I stumbled upon the legendary karuvaadu (Tamil for dried fish) market at the end of Wall Tax Road. And then there was the Kasimedu fish market on Sundays that I visited a few times: once with a friend and their father, and later by myself (for research) to watch women cut fish heads on an arivalmanai, a kind of horizontal sharp knife sat on a wooden base, like a steel swan ready for the sacrifice.

But these were places that weren't frequented by my family. There was no talk of salted fish and chicken curry for dinner, nor was beef biryani served at weddings. Instead, there was a hierarchy of purity to be followed within my household – washing hands before touching the vessel containing yoghurt or ghee, plates only to be kept on a specified surface in the kitchen, certain spoons became out of bounds for dishes containing onion and garlic . . . eating together at home was regimented. Our diet consisted of vegetables, beans, lentils, veggie curries and endless amounts of rice. Local newspapers decreed Chennai a vegetarian haven, and would have contests judging restaurants serving the best (vegetarian) tiffin of idli-vadai-sambar-filter-coffee year after year. A newspaper publication I worked at as a sub-editor issued a notice asking us to not bring 'non-vegetarian food' into the canteens, citing 'discomfort to the majority of the employees who are vegetarian'. In Chennai, even lunch was contested.

I wrote about this notice, along with the other ways that the country I grew up in discriminates against 'non-vegetarians', for my newsletter in 2020.[1] The word non-vegetarian is a unique Indian coinage, standing in for both meat eaters and meat itself; the prefix indicates vegetarianism's normative status in the country, while also reducing meat (and its eaters) to be less conspicuous,[2] even if only 39 per cent of Indian adults call themselves vegetarian.[3] This food hierarchy, created by a powerful minority, classifies vegetarian food as being the 'pure', 'good' and the norm – as opposed to 'non-vegetarian' food as being 'impure', 'bad' and 'lower in status'. While access, availability, local cuisines and food habits form one part of the story, it is the political and cultural factors that tie up the rest. It is caste, religion and gender that gatekeep what foods can be (and are) consumed by which group.

Food is as much a source of exclusion, transgression and hegemony as it is a source of inclusion and community. And nothing embodies this better than commensality – that favourite anthropological concept considered as being central to social organisation, rituals, kinship, social and political relations, and cosmologies even. Commensality, from commensal, or eating together, from the Latin words *com* (meaning together) and *mensa* (meaning table or meal on the table), is substance of kinship and fellowship of the table; it's feasting from the common pot, the organisation of social relations.

Yet it is also about power at the table, gastro-politics and disharmony – the idea that bounded bodies come together for and with food is sometimes challenging, especially in a country where one's identity is based on what one cooks and eats. The myth of India as a vegetarian nation isn't unfounded – it comes from a food hierarchy created by those who define themselves as vegetarians and have accorded the diet its normative status in the country. Food identities in this country, like religion and caste, all of which are tied together in the history of structural inequality, are a form of inheritance. What my grandparents ate is what my parents ate is what my sister and I ate. Eat. And are still eating. And it is true for most Indians: the impact of dietary choices on the environment aside, diets here are usually informed by tradition, religion, local culture, social divisions, hierarchies and families.

Sometimes it's hard to see what is right in front of us, not because it's invisible, but because it has been rendered as such. Although I realised early on that consuming meat wasn't 'impure', it took me longer – twenty-five years – to actually eat it. I tried to dissociate myself from my family's obsessive view of meat and purity taboos. In Chennai, and later in London, I piled on the meat – chicken 65, roast beef, sausage, lamb, chicken rasam, offal – in a hope that I could find a small window into what my life could have been like. I had already stopped going to the temple when I turned eighteen; I didn't think of myself as god-fearing anyway. Like Chitrita Banerjee, I too 'found myself even more distanced from the celebratory, worshipful life of my childhood'.[4]

But the ability to switch to and from mindless moral considerations is a privilege in itself. To afford and be able to eat meat confers a status upon the person eating it, but like everything else in the country, that status depends on your caste and religion. Consumption of beef (and pork) is closely linked to caste status,[5] and to lynching and bans in several states – linked further to Hindu upper caste sentiments. Eggs, which are nutritious and vegetarian in the rest of the world, have been awarded a 'non-vegetarian' status here, and frequently omitted from government noon-meal schemes for school children in many states. This war against meat is different then; it's not about convincing people to consume less beef or pork, introducing nuance into conversations surrounding the ethics of meat eating or its impact on the environment. It's a war on *who* consumes it, *who* survives on it, and *whose* social dynamics are affected by it.

My social dynamics certainly weren't affected by my decision to eat meat. I had (and still have) the access to good quality cuts of meat, and the privilege to eat meat without being questioned about it, let alone my life being in danger for eating what would simply be a satiating dinner. But eating meat did help me rethink food in terms of politics. Why was it easy for me to be vegetarian all my life, and then to take the decision to eat meat? Like some of my friends and family, I have the benefit of caste hierarchy on my side as a vegetarian Brahmin growing up in middle-class Chennai. The inheritance of my identity – foremost my religion and caste – means that I haven't been discriminated against for a school or college seat. Nor have I been refused a house to rent because of what I consumed, or what my name was.

So I decided to disinherit a few things. The once-transparent caste bubble of my childhood now reveals superficial customs that I question every chance I get. The idea of an arranged marriage that my parents so badly wanted for me, and which I never considered since turning eighteen, has been put to rest after a year-long argument. I have realised that eating for pleasure does not have to be loaded with guilt but that I do have to recognise the labour systems that helped bring the food onto my plate. I have learned to have conversations about caste within the expanse of my home, among close and extended family, even if the result is that I do not get invited to events and celebrations anymore. I've also realised that I'm in no position to lead this particular conversation. Instead, I'm trying to be more open-hearted and reflective; be more accountable, speak up and question structures; acknowledge my Brahmin privilege; and disinherit casteist and religious habits, customs and practices that no longer serve me.

The act of consumption in a casteist society, when you see it, can shake you up in ways that you hadn't anticipated. It can make you aware of the structures of production and distribution, of social and cosmological developments, and class and caste hierarchies as well. Indian food, which is linked closely to the moral and social status of individuals and groups, is rarely analysed in terms of labour systems. For the farmers in Delhi, whose year-long protest against the hostile agricultural laws successfully ended in December 2021, it was a fight for their livelihood. When the central government tried to dismantle structures that had been in place for decades and would leave everyone vulnerable, besides increasing the 'already most unjust imbalance of power between farmers and the giant corporations they will be dealing with', it wasn't a rural agrarian crisis anymore.[6] It was about sustenance: a matter of life and death.

Caste privilege helped me build an independent life, find work, and to just go about life unbothered. The school I went to didn't treat me any different than my other Brahmin and upper caste classmates even when I performed badly or when I refused to obey rules. I was allowed to eat what I wanted for lunch – and why wouldn't I be, since I was a vegetarian? Some of my friends, on the other hand, were reprimanded for bringing a couple of hard-boiled eggs in their lunch boxes, hidden beneath a mound of rice. This is the same caste privilege that helped me study in London, obtain a loan and slowly pay it back. It also helped me re-assimilate after I came back home. To not worry about rent and food in the middle of a pandemic isn't just a blessing, it is a privilege for which I will always be grateful. This is my inheritance: my privilege handed down from the past to the present, and which by its own nature has given me the luxury of disinheritance. It has defined me, even as I am actively redefining it now. And just like my mother's preserved salted lime pickle, I will pass it on.

Still Standing: Field Notes on Removed Confederate Statues

Duron Chavis

It was recently reported in the *New York Times* that my city, Richmond, Virginia, has a 'complicated past' because we're now 'devoid of Confederate statues' which means we're entering a 'compelling new chapter'.[1] As a Black native Richmonder and a farmer who has dedicated his entire life to Black liberation strategies through food, this complicated past and compelling new chapter looks no different to the time when those statues were still standing.

At first glance, one might feel compelled to celebrate the removal of these relics of the Lost Cause mythology. During the zeitgeist of the George Floyd rebellions across the country, these statues were razed by protesters, vandalised, and became sites for selfies, graffiti and community protest. In Richmond, the location of the Robert E. Lee statue was renamed the Marcus-David Peters Circle in remembrance of a young Black man who was murdered by police during a mental health crisis. The fact that these statues could even exist in the first place tells a story of power; a story much deeper than has been told: that taking down Confederate statues does absolutely nothing to upset the balance of power or who has it in the city.

Monument Avenue and those who live on this stretch of street in the former capital of the Confederacy are a living testament to the scars of slavery and colonialism. This part of Richmond is predominantly white. The median house price at the time of writing is $1.6 million.[2] The roads are made of cobblestone. Those that live there are only two or three blocks away from science museums, art museums and history museums. Minus the statues, one might be hard-pressed to find another relic of racism on this road beyond its predominant whiteness, but one has to look no further than its abundant tree cover to reveal that story. It's hidden in plain sight, but you have to do a little research to understand why.

Redlining, a systemic racist housing policy that was practised in the 1950s, denied Black and brown neighbourhoods access to federal dollars for mortgages and loans, and led to the divestment of Black neighbourhoods. The divestment was so bad you can now predict which neighbourhoods will be hotter – and neighbourhoods like Monument Avenue will be cooler, due to them having an established tree canopy. The historically Black neighbourhoods that people who look like me grew up in had been covered in impervious surfaces and lacked green infrastructure. To quote Lil Wayne: 'Tha Block Is [quite literally] Hot'.

Take Gilpin Court, for example. The housing project

located in a formerly redlined neighbourhood in Richmond is literally five to twelve degrees hotter than Monument Avenue in the summer due to its lack of trees and greenery.[3] People living in this neighbourhood have a life expectancy of sixty-three years, but in Westover Hills (a white neighbourhood) that number is eighty-three.[4] A twenty-year difference in life expectancy. The latest state investment in Gilpin Court was new cameras for police supervision. There is a pool, but that has been closed for ten years.

We often speak about redlining and housing discrimination. We rarely draw the line connecting that phenomenon to slavery and colonisation. Such connections are expected to be inferred. It was easy to make that connection by pointing to those statues. Their removal does not increase the life expectancy in Gilpin Court, nor does it cool down how hot it gets there in the summer.

I like my racism clear and undisguised. I remember going to protest against the alt-right using a public library for one of their meetings when I was in my mid-twenties. I will never forget my expectations: redneck, flannel shirts, bearded white men with cut-off sleeves, and Confederate flag patches emblazoned on the backs of tattered jean jackets. What I saw was a clean-cut white man in a suit and tie surrounded by rightfully angry Black people as he calmly articulated that he felt white people were the superior race and that Black people came from monkeys.

With the Confederate statues up, it was easier to describe how systems of oppression are the by-product of policies that have been created by and implemented by white people to the disadvantage of Black and brown people. I had something I could show you that clearly demonstrated inequity.

The racism was loud. Clear. Sitting atop a horse. On a pillar and pointing west in allusion to Manifest Destiny. In your face. Undisguised. Just like the racism of that alt-right guy in the suit and tie. It shouted its racism unapologetically.

The erecting of a statue is a policy decision. Land use has to be considered. Who owns the land the statue will stand on? Who will pay for it to be built? How tall can it be? What can the statue be representative of? If that statue is of someone who had committed treason against the government, how can it be left standing for over one hundred years? These are policy decisions implemented by white people for white people.

How about the act of redlining and its subsequent housing discrimination? A policy that was implemented by the same white people who had erected those statues. The slave trade and Jim Crow discrimination? USDA discrimination against Black farmers? A policy that had been implemented by white people to their benefit to the disadvantage of Black people. The social construct of racism perpetuates systems that continue to privilege white people and disadvantage Black people based on an intricate web of policy decisions. Tracing racist ideas down to who thought them and who created the policy that mirrors them is important because it teaches us they are not gods. New ideas can take shape. New policies can be implemented. Change can be made when we understand how things got to where they are today.

Alas, the Confederate statues that delineated the truth of Richmond, VA's past policies as the capital of the Confederacy are no more. The ease with which we could point at those statues to extol the continued lording over of Black and brown people by the ideals of a losing Confederacy has drifted into distant memory. The hard work of connecting those dots now lies at our feet, and in my case, as a farmer – beneath.

It is fascinating to hear white people, especially tourism industry buffs, gush ravenously over the Black-owned restaurants that one can visit in Richmond now that those pesky Confederate statues are gone, but these restaurants were always here. The presence of Black people cooking in the city is not a new phenomenon. In urban cities, from slavery to Jim Crow, Black-run kitchens have always existed. One could argue that the history of American Southern food was written by Black people. From crops that were brought to the US via slavery, to the enslaved hands that grew them, to the actual cooking and culinary artistry being done by Black people – Black people and food are not strangers in the South. The Civil War was fought to keep my ancestors cooking, growing and working FOR white people.

One stark difference between the past and now is that between Reconstruction and the present day Black people have lost over 12 million acres of land. Where does the food that Black restaurants use to cook come from in the context of Black farmers losing $325 billion of land value over the past century? Who stole the land from Black folk? How did our radical imagining during a global rebellion against police brutality stall at the removal of Confederate statues, while 98 per cent of American farmland is still owned by white people?[5] As a farmer that was born in the city, I deal with this question intimately every day. Where is the land I can farm on? Who owns it? I also work as an educator to teach my community about food systems. In a working food system, you have production, aggregation, innovation and distribution.

Someone gets paid every step of the way. The removal of Robert E. Lee's statue does not grant me better control over the food system in my community.

Land is the basis for power and self-determination. Across the globe Black people are resisting, strategising and building alternative food systems that are owned and controlled by the progeny of the formerly enslaved and colonised. White supremacy mandates that we are the labour force in every aspect of the food system. It mandates that we work the land for the benefit of white people. The taking down of Confederate statues does not disrupt this relationship.

The removal of Confederate statues does not transform my landlessness into land ownership and repossession. It does not bring fresh fruits and vegetables to Black communities concentrated in poverty. It does not provide affordable housing and green infrastructure to my community. It doesn't stop fentanyl overdoses or gun violence. It doesn't plant trees in housing projects. I don't even drive down Monument Avenue. The West End of Richmond, Virginia is predominantly white.

The historically Black neighbourhoods in this city were Jackson Ward, the Northside, Southside and East End of Richmond. All formerly redlined neighbourhoods. All lacking in access to healthy food. All hotter than Monument Avenue in the summer. I was born on Southside, like my mother and my father. My wife is from Northside. My grandfather and great grandmother are both from Northside.

The monuments we have built for ourselves in our lifetime were transformed from vacant lots on the Southside into urban farms filled with murals and solar panels. The trees we have planted to give shade and food to others and ourselves. The soil we have improved the fertility of by using compost bins and manure from chickens. The rows we have tilled into a hundred feet of growing African crops like okra, scotch bonnet peppers and callaloo.

A temple in a housing project was erected in tree plantings, raised beds and permeable pathways because it lacked access to healthy food and biophilic places for children to play. A shrine was established in a formerly redlined neighbourhood in the form of a community garden with shade structures to serve as oasis for folks struggling with concentrated poverty and lack of green space.

These were living statues that taught food justice and climate resiliency. We painted Fannie Lou Hamer, George Jackson, Amilcar Cabral, Claudia Jones and George Washington Carver on twenty-four-foot-long free-standing mural walls, built by our own callused hands on land we reclaimed in the name of our ancestors. We welded metal statues of sankofa birds there, next to shipping containers we had converted into tool sheds and covered with visuals commissioned by Black artists.

In Northside we erected greenhouses to produce seedlings, youth farms and pop-ups like the Northside Farmers Market, a community-led effort committed to purchasing food from Black farmers by organisations and residents of Northside. My aunt-in-law tells me that our home in Northside had a cross burned in its front lawn in the fifties because they were one of the first Black families who had moved to this formerly predominantly white side of town, abandoned by white flight and blockbusting. Our monuments reflect our hope and dreams for tomorrow.

The way forward is meandering and iterative, yet not

complicated or next chapter-esque. It's the same as it has always been. Our policy has been Black self-determination and agency. Our adversaries – those who built the Confederate monuments – have worked against that for us. The folks who mandated that those statues should go up still maintain power in Richmond, Virginia.

How do we build regenerative monuments to Black liberation in the former capital of the Confederacy? We have only just begun planting the seeds of this revolution.

Serving Up Sisterhood: The Power of Black Feminism, Food and Freedom

Tambra Raye Stevenson, MPH, MA

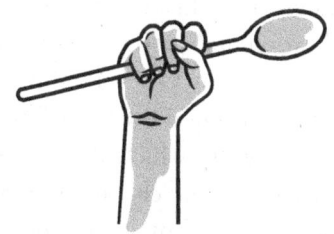

My Search for Sisterhood: From Soil to Soul

As a first-generation Oklahoma State University (OSU) student, I sought academic success and sisterhood. My first encounter with sisterhood was through the Alpha Kappa Alpha Sorority, Inc. It wasn't just a sorority; it was a promise of a bond, a unified force that transcended mere friendship. This connection would provide solace and strength during the challenges ahead, shaping my formative years.

Alpha Kappa Alpha Sorority, Inc.'s official colours, apple green and salmon pink, symbolise the abundance of life, womanliness, fidelity and love. For the love of community, our beloved sorority sisters dedicate their life and legacy of service to Black family, health, arts, education and global impact, which deeply resonated with my ideals. My high school principal, Dr Silvya Kirk, who embodied strength and leadership, is a member. My cousin Kristie's sorority experiences at the Oklahoma State University also solidified my resolve to join. As fate would have it, during my first year, I crossed paths with two kind-hearted members who left a lasting impression. Their gestures, although simple, were indicative of the larger ethos of the sorority. No obstacle would be insurmountable if I had sisters like these by my side.

Through dedication and passion, I ascended to chapter president of my sorority at OSU. Leading initiatives like our health fair and chairing the scholarship programme as part of Think Pink Week, which is a week of service in honour of the sorority and chapter founders and their ideals, allowed me to serve my community and provided opportunities to forge deeper bonds with my sisters. Later, as an OSU alumnus, I went on to create the Women Advancing Nutrition Dietetics and Agriculture (WANDA) Endowed Scholarship to increase representation and support for women of African descent in the field. I expanded the WANDA Scholar Program to Kano, Nigeria in partnership with local non-governmental organisations supporting forty-five women to date at Bayero University in overcoming financial hardship and reducing the risk of human trafficking. From coast to coast, wherever I found myself, I could always rely on a sister from the sorority.

The legacy of sisterhood lives on in our commitment to one another and the cause we hold dear. And as bell hooks rightly reminds us: 'Solidarity is not the same as support. To experience solidarity, we must have a community of interests, shared beliefs, and goals around which to unite, to build Sisterhood. Support can be occasional. It can be given and just as easily withdrawn. Solidarity requires sustained, ongoing commitment.[1] It's not just about support but the enduring commitment to a shared goal. However, a troubling pattern emerged as I delved deeper into agriculture, dietetics, nutrition and food. The collective identity of sisterhood that I had so profoundly cherished was notably absent. The overwhelming loneliness and underrepresentation in these domains were palpable, and I yearned for that familiar embrace of sisterhood. So, I set out on a vision of a united front of Black women, a sisterhood of fierce food sheroes championing the cause of health and nutrition. Thus, my quest for serving up sisterhood truly began.

From the Heart: Healing Souls in the Kitchens and Soils

The clinking of pots and pans, the rhythmic chopping of vegetables, and turning on the radio for some soul music are all familiar sounds in a kitchen. For many, the kitchen is a sanctuary, a place of creation and nourishment. Yet for some Black women in America, the history of the kitchen is a beautiful quilt with patchworks threaded with both trauma and triumph.

For example, the antebellum South is filled with stories of Black women toiling in plantation kitchens, our sweat mixing with the spices as we prepared meals for our oppressors. Our bodies were exploited, our souls suppressed, yet our spirits were unyielding. The kitchens, while sites of subjugation, became covert meeting places where the seeds of rebellion were sown.

This complex duality is intrinsic to the discourse of Black feminism. Historically, Black feminism has asserted agency in the face of systemic oppression. It champions intersectionality, recognising that the oppressions faced by Black women are unique, born out of both race and gender. But how does this relate to food and freedom?

Throughout history, Black women have harnessed the power of food as a tool for resistance and liberation. Feeding freedom movements, Georgia Gilmore created the underground kitchen that became a fundraising hub in the throes of the civil rights movement.[2] Her culinary prowess satisfied palates like that of Dr Martin Luther King, Jr. and fuelled the Montgomery Bus Boycott. While navigating the Underground Railroad, Harriet Tubman used cooking to fund her livelihood and relied on her knowledge of natural foods to nourish those seeking freedom from slavery. Fannie Lou Hamer championed food sovereignty, believing that access to food was integral to the civil rights struggle.[3] Then we have Dr Wangari Maathai, who planted trees through the collective power of women to heal Mama Africa. These remarkable women exemplify how food can be a powerful tool for liberation.

Now more than ever, Black women are redefining our relationship with kitchens and food by transforming spaces once marked by trauma into sites of cultural reclamation and empowerment. Using ancestral recipes and sustainable practices, they foster community, health, and food justice. Black women are exploring how their food can be their medicine by remixing traditional recipes for health benefits. For instance, instead of boiling greens, we sauté or turn them into salads and smoothies. It's no longer about subservience but about reclaiming spaces and narratives. The kitchen has metamorphosed into a healing ground where Black women can nourish our bodies and souls, drawing strength from our rich heritage.

Sisterhood from the soil to the soul is cultivated as Black women gather around kitchen tables to share meals made from produce grown on their communal land, blending stories, recipes and gardening tips that nourish both their bodies and their spirits. From crops to cuisine, food has always been a unifier, a medium through which stories are passed down, traditions are upheld and cultures are celebrated. But now, these gatherings aren't just about sharing meals; they are about sharing missions. I dream of a world where Black women as a collective use our superpowers as food sheroes to manifest a vision of healthier, equitable communities through shared knowledge, cultural wisdom and mutual support.

As COVID-19 ravaged communities, Black women faced the Herculean task of safeguarding our families' health by transforming into meal healers, cultural keepers and culinary creators. Sisterhood Suppers, pioneered by WANDA, became a sacred space for sharing stories of self-care and social change, for transcending, cooking and growing food. The Sisterhood Suppers have become a cherished community tradition, especially during Juneteenth, as a way to reclaim Freedom Day and to advocate for food justice and celebrate food freedom fighters in our communities. Together we enjoy the delicious discussions delving into self-love, power of sisterhood, and serving our community using food. In these grounded gatherings, women found solace, nourishment, solidarity and strategies to challenge and change the status quo.

The inequities in health outcomes are glaring. Chronic diseases are rampant, and in many Black communities, one's zip code dictates life expectancy more than one's genetic code. This isn't mere coincidence; it's a consequence of entrenched systemic inequities from policies to the press, a manifestation of food apartheid. If Black women are to rewrite this narrative, they must transition from passive consumers to active food citizens. The key isn't just in our kitchens but in our voices and our votes.

Paula Giddings underscores the significance of Black women's narratives as she states: 'That is why for a Black woman to write about Black women is at once a personal and an objective undertaking.'[4] To write about Black women is to uncover layers of histories, struggles and triumphs. It's about illuminating paths trodden and charting unexplored journeys. In the ever-evolving narrative of Black feminism, food and freedom, the message is clear. Affirmed by our histories, fortified by our sisterhoods, and inspired by our visions, Black women must be at the forefront of a food revolution; because the stakes are high and we have most to lose as it pertains to food and nutrition security. So let's turn the hunger pains into a powerful movement for change, because we are the food sheroes that our communities need.

Reclaiming Our Space: The Genesis of WANDA and the Power of Intersectional Sisterhood

In a world where the pressure to fit in often blurs the lines of individuality, I consistently found myself on the periphery, the square peg in a round hole. Being a Black woman brought the complexities of intersecting identities – class, geography, race, gender – all of which seemed to layer upon me like an intricate tapestry. Within these layered identities, I was marginalised, excluded, and perpetually feeling like an outsider.

Diaspora African Women's Network founder Semhar Araia's words resonated deeply with me: Create the spaces you wish existed.[5] So, I set forth to create spaces when none seemed welcoming. It was a clarion call to take charge of a collective narrative and collective image makeover of Black women in food, where Black women could stand unapologetically in our truth and be seen and heard as the queens of greens that they are. Thus, WANDA was born – a manifestation of my longing, a platform to celebrate our uniqueness, and a space to be ourselves in every sense.

Audre Lorde's profound reflections on the intricacies of Black women's experiences laid the foundation for WANDA's ethos:

> We have to consciously study how to be tender with each other until it becomes a habit because what was native has been stolen from us, the love of Black women for each other. But we can practice being gentle with each other by being gentle with that piece of ourselves that is hardest to hold, by giving more to the brave bruised girlchild within each of us, and by expecting a little less from her enormous efforts to excel. We can love her in the light and darkness, quiet her frenzy toward perfection, and encourage her attention toward fulfillment . . . As we arm ourselves with ourselves and each other, we can stand toe to toe inside that rigorous loving and begin to speak the impossible – or what has always seemed like the impossible – to one

another... Eventually, if we speak the truth to each other, it will become unavoidable to ourselves.[6]

Audre Lorde's poignant words encapsulate the essence of this journey. Loving ourselves, being gentle with our internal struggles and leaning into sisterhood became paramount. It was evident that the salvation of one Black woman was inextricably linked to the collective upliftment of all. WANDA became more than just an organisation; it became a movement of mamas, aunties, nanas and sisters with a call to arms proclaiming, 'I am WANDA. We are WANDA.'

By embracing an intersectional framework, WANDA sought to delve deep into the multi-faceted experiences of Black women. Recognising that narratives of race or gender weren't enough, WANDA aimed to dissect the interlocking systems of oppression that impede our progress. Through this lens, we found kinship with Black feminist organisations like the Combahee River Collective, whose manifesto resonated with our beliefs and vision.

WANDA's mission is simple yet profound: to build a pipeline from farm to health, where women and girls become the food sheroes that our communities need. As custodians of culture and reservoirs of healing wisdom, we have a shared legacy to uphold and pass on. It's a recognition of the sacrifices of our ancestors and an acknowledgement that our existence today is a testament to our resilience. It's a vow to resist continuously and a commitment to find healing moments amid the resistance.

By converging Black women food leaders, WANDA works tirelessly to eradicate food apartheid in our communities by reclaiming space in policy and media that shapes the discourse and enables us to thrive. That's why WANDA launched a food democracy study and issued a policy report to the White House Conference on Hunger, Nutrition, and Health, where we advocated for a Food Bill of Rights in 2022. Additionally, we are developing a Food Citizens Guide to empower everyday people to take collective action. To heal our communities and eradicate food apartheid begins with emancipating and reclaiming our minds and souls from the colonial gaze; then the rest shall follow.

We Rise: The Collective Culinary Odyssey of Black Women

Maya Angelou's poetic resonance captures the essence of Black feminism – a movement that has historically intertwined with the language of food; her words in 'Still I Rise' speak to my soul.[7] For Black women, cooking and nurturing are spiritual, political and revolutionary, embodying the spirit of ubuntu – our interconnectedness and shared humanity, recognising that *I am because we are.*

The kitchens we know today, laden with aromas of soul food from Africa and the diaspora, and memories of gatherings, were not always safe havens. Our ancestors witnessed them as spaces of subjugation and pain. But with resilience and determination, Black women are transforming these spaces, instilling them with the philosophy of communalism – that our nourishment and well-being are intricately tied to the collective.

However, this isn't just about historical reflection but a call to action for the present and future. As the world demands our food, agriculture and nutrition expertise, we must create platforms where Black women take centre stage. Rooted deeply in the wisdom of our ancestors, we envision a future of vibrant health.

So to every Black woman out there, know this: you are the continuation of a divine feminine legacy, the embodiment of centuries of struggle, triumph, and the prayers manifested before you joined us on Mother Earth. Stand firm in the soil like a sunflower soaking the power of the sun rays beaming your brilliance and illuminating your path. Together, as Black women united in purpose and in the spirit of ubuntu, we're not just dreaming of a brighter, healthier future; we're cooking up change, serving it one delicious dish at a time.

Neuro Spicy: Overlooked and Undervalued, the Dismissal of ADHD Traits in the Workplace

Zoe Adjonyoh

I found out I had ADHD when I was forty-four years old. Me. A grown-ass accomplished and 'successful' woman, a 'celebrity' chef, an author (who actually wrote their own cookbook, as flawed as it may have been) and an entrepreneur no less, discovering she has ADHD in her mid-forties is giving all kinds of overwhelm.

I found out by accident. I had just started my position as director of women's leadership programmes at the James Beard Foundation. Tasked with creating a three-year strategy and closing the gender pay gap for women in hospitality, it was no small job ahead of me. There was a HUGE expectation placed on me as their 'rock star' chef employee. The only person on the payroll at the time who was actively working in hospitality. I was up for the challenge. After being

CEO of my own two businesses for the preceding thirteen years and already a thought leader in the space, I came armed with an artillery of creative problem-solving solutions and a keen head for big sky thinking. Secure in my integrity, I was sure I would thrive. I was excited to 'make a difference'.

I've always been addicted to personal development. From the business realm to the spiritual and all in between, I have a battalion of courses, short and long, under my belt to prove it. Everything from NLP life coaching with Tony Robbins to Kundalini yoga training, herbalism, tarot and astrology to digital marketing and social media courses, integrating AI into standard operating systems, with many business accelerators in between. It's the Scorpio in me, the deep desire to unearth the truth of who we are and why.

I'm a master at shadow work at this point – it's been a daily ritual since I began my healing journey. And I've taken every personality test you can think of. I'm an eight on the enneagram. I'm a rainmaker. I'm a Manifesting Generator in human design, yadda yadda . . . and let's not even get me started on my life path number and birth chart. As the eponymous 'Black Sheep', I have been seeking the truth of who I am and what makes me tick my entire life. So when I was told upon joining JBF that everyone had to complete a DiSC® assessment test for the benefit of understanding colleagues' work styles better, I was excited. Yeah, I'm that geek. I was excited. I wanted to know the people I'd be working with better and how to help motivate or encourage them and for them to know me in the same way.

I was a Di. The dissection of what this meant was like therapy for me: people whose DiSC® profile shows a Di style display both the dominance of the 'D' style and the influence of the 'i' style. They are persuasive, bold, and results-oriented. They like to move fast and are always looking for new opportunities. People with Di styles are often viewed as dynamic and outspoken.[1]

Okaayyyy. Of course my lower ego was getting pumped reading this. Sounds familiar and wonderful so far . . .

Traits: Active, results-oriented, vocal, enthusiastic, assertive, quick, dynamic, inquisitive, persuasive, rebellious, restless, colourful, charming, intimidating, bold, driven, entrepreneurial.

Driven by: Quick action, new opportunities.

Anxieties: Loss of power, loss of status, invisibility *(ouch, but yes, true)*.

Influences others by: Charm, bold action.

In tense situations: Addresses issues head-on, may say things they will regret.

Let me just highlight this part: *may say things they will regret.*

Oooh chile. If I had a penny . . .

It revealed a lot of complexity about myself that I thought was useful intel both for my personal and leadership growth and I felt reassured that my line manager would also read it to better know how to manage and encourage me. *I'm not easy to manage.* A former colleague later shared that this was the narrative that had been asserted about me. It's fair.

The day never came when my line manager found the time or inclination to read my test results, though I had devoured theirs and my co-workers in a bid to understand my new environment and colleagues. As my requests to have that informed insight be part of our working relationship were repeatedly set aside, I understood what their personality was and made accommodations. I took what I could from it and used it to 'improve' myself.

The quest took a left turn when the results from the

DiSC® sent me on a deep dive which resulted in me taking the Adverse Childhood Experiences (ACE) test.

The test lays out ten questions that indicate the levels of trauma you might face from unresolved childhood trauma. I scored ten out of ten on the test. According to Ace Aware, if the ACE score is 1–3 with ACE-Associated Health Conditions, the patient is at 'intermediate risk'. If the ACE score is 4 or higher, even without ACE-associated health conditions, the patient is at 'high risk' for toxic stress physiology.[2]

> Did you know that herbal supplements like ginkgo biloba, ginseng and chamomile are believed to enhance cognitive function, reduce anxiety and improve attention span?

ACEs include all types of abuse and neglect, such as parental substance use, incarceration and domestic violence. ACEs can also include situations that may cause trauma for a child, such as having a parent with a mental illness or being part of a family going through a divorce. There is a significant relationship between a high ACE score and ADHD: the more adverse childhood experiences, the higher the risk of having moderate to severe ADHD. 'In their research Felitti et al. found that adults who had experienced 4 or more ACEs showed a 12 times higher prevalence of health risks such as alcoholism, drug use, depression, and suicide attempts. These findings raised awareness about the connection between childhood experiences and outcomes as an adult.'[3]

> **❝** Did you know that omega-3 fatty acids found in fatty cold-water fish such as salmon, tuna and mackerel or in walnuts, chia seeds and flaxseed provide the proteins which are the building blocks of our neurotransmitters like dopamine? They can support brain health and may improve attention and cognitive function. **❞**

The results of this then took me down a rabbit hole of self-testing. I took various tests for PTSD and bipolar disorder and finally ADHD and AuADHD (autism and ADHD). I took them all and it shook out that I'd likely had all of these my whole life.

It wasn't the PTSD or bipolar that shocked me – they felt like an inevitable diagnosis I had been avoiding in favour of self-medicating in destructive ways; people pleasing, toxic self-dependency, workaholism, alcoholism and drug dependency. Shout out to all the chefs who have existed in this toxicity as part of the 'chef lifestyle' and broken free. (I've been in recovery since April 2020.)

I had exorcised the worst of my demons and toxic and abusive relationships. I had thought I was doing OK – especially since being sober.

It was the ADHD that hit me like a tonne of bricks. So much made sense suddenly. A life of anxiety and depression. A life of being demonised for always being late and missing appointments. Always juggling multiple projects simultaneously without the physical resources to do so. Struggling with rejection. 'Over-sensitivity'. Being called scatter-brained, and unable to focus on tasks that were unstimulating to me. An inability to distribute tasks to a team because all the information was in my mind and I didn't know how to prioritise sharing the information. So I kept it locked inside my brain and took on too much, only adding to the overwhelm.

My executive function was a hot mess. The number of times my team at Zoe's Ghana Kitchen in London implored me to focus on the restaurant and drop the events and street food. They didn't need to mention I should drop the unpaid 'exposure' that was taking up so much of my time yet not bringing in customers. I knew it was distracting me from the restaurant's success, but I just couldn't focus on one thing. I needed the other parts of the cog to be able to turn every day. I was hopeless at spreadsheets. It took SO MUCH energy to be able to put together a simple spreadsheet. Not because it was hard to do, but because it was simply impossible for my neural pathways to want to pay attention to the task. I had a frustrated wife who always had to remind me of appointments, and friends who had to suffer my late or non-replies to text messages or emails which I forgot to respond to because I got distracted. And did I mention I wouldn't eat unless it was in my schedule to do so, or a meal was provided for me? I could feed an army as a chef but easily forget to feed myself routinely.

> Did you know protein-rich foods including lean meats, legumes and dairy products in the diet provide a steady release of energy and help maintain focus and concentration?

I had lived with it because I just assumed that's how everyone's brain worked. A running commentary of every sense and nuance that was happening or needed to happen. I saw a tweet that said 'Habits, for me, are things that I can reliably remember to do. I have a procedure, I go through it, I'm familiar with every step. That apparently is not what neurotypical folks get to experience. They don't have to *decide* to do them. They don't have to *remember* to do them. Things just happen automatically because they've done enough to engage and make them automatic.'[4] My mind was blown. What? You mean to tell me this isn't normal? I have to set reminders to eat and hydrate on a timer otherwise it won't happen. And I've been a chef for thirteen years!

There was a time I used to think that ADHD only applied to children. I thought it meant a child was hyperactive and that it was specifically used for boys. Their parents gave them too much sugar or Coke. It turns out that studies on ADHD were only done on boys and that was the narrative that was pushed out. Women and girls can present very differently. We have become so good at hiding our ADHD traits because the misogyny and patriarchy teach us to be 'good girls', be nice and polite and not a nuisance to anyone. Women are in fact so good at managing their hyper-vigilance and masking, they get misdiagnosed with anxiety and depression or PMS. We are living in a constant state of overwhelm, with crippling low self-esteem, struggling to maintain relationships, and are ultra-sensitive to rejection and we don't know why. Don't even get me started on ADHD paralysis and 'productive procrastination' tendencies – like interviewing every mentor and mentee of a platform no one is using or cares about to prove it is not worthwhile to keep it. When it came to large event cooking, I often found myself unable to unload the stress of a service and this manifested in brain freeze, short temperedness and lack of direction for the team; my brain was paralysed with a lack of ability to make a decision or share it once made. It was difficult for my team to deal with my ping pong brain and my consequent frustration.

Believe it or not, social interactions were also a challenge. I can either give you perfect eye contact or have my brain actively engaging in what you're saying. You can't have both. So if we meet for the first time, and you tell me your name – if I'm giving you perfect eye contact there is zero chance I will remember your name. It's why when I'm in large virtual meetings, I prefer to have my camera turned off so I can focus on what people are saying. The more it looks like I'm not paying attention to you, in fact the more I'm actually paying attention to what you're saying.

> **❝** Did you know that caffeine, in moderation, found in coffee and tea, can increase alertness and focus? However, moderation is key to avoid overstimulation and sleep disturbances. **❞**

I had already switched to decaf coffee around the time of sobriety; however, switching to mushroom coffee was a real game changer in terms of alertness and focus, reserving my decaf coffee for just one cup in the morning as opposed to the six cups of coffee and ten cups of tea before noon which used to comprise my morning 'breakfast'. Decaf tea was helpful in balancing the energy of my mind – especially herbal teas, including valerian root, ginkgo, lion's mane and ginger. I learned through herbalism it's a good idea to play around with mixing and matching what works for you as one size never fits all. As a chef it's another fun way to bridge the art and science of 'cooking' and for me it's a natural extension of the mission behind promoting the health benefits of single-origin spices from West Africa.

Defiance rings true here, since I was also that truth teller and truth speaker (food activism) who would rarely bow to the conventions or paradigms others felt obliged to follow in pursuit of their careers. I gave respect where it was earned, not by default. I followed rules that made sense to me, not purely because they existed. I would call out festival directors, food halls, brands and publications for any scheme or contract that intended to shortchange, disempower or improperly compensate me. I did this directly to their face and on public platforms. My colleagues seemed to bemoan the shortcomings of the industry in private, complaining about the state of things in the privacy of their group chats and social gatherings, while I took a fog horn and made my complaints loud and clear on public platforms. This is why so many people called upon me to 'get involved' in disputes in public. I was constantly tagged into discussions of cultural appropriation or where under-represented people were being shortchanged. I was the poster girl for revolt in the food industry. *But they knew that when they hired me . . .*

This was the energy behind the Black Book initiative in 2020, which was centred on decolonising the food industry and discussing all these issues in a public forum with an international food community and audience.[5] No one else was doing this at the time, hence its success – for a limited time. I later realised that my undiagnosed ADHD had been a factor in this project's unbecoming, along with a lack of willingness within the industry to explore and effect REAL change beyond the virtue-signalling micro moves made in the wake of George Floyd's brutal murder in police custody.

So it was the ADHD that hit me like a tonne of bricks. Being neuro spicy alerted me to how much unprocessed trauma is stored in my body. On top of this overwhelming news I had a legitimate rationale behind my very individual work style and process. I had a legitimate reason for my so-called shortcomings. I was stunned. Stunned into grief for all the pain of having done things the hard way for so long. Without help. Without knowledge of self. I was also overwhelmed with how this diagnosis was going to affect my new role as I was already out of step with the organisation's company 'culture' of excessive meetings and what seemed like illogical and unnecessary processes, deadlines and workflows.

It didn't feel entirely safe to bring it up as an issue at work. I had witnessed the bombastic side-eye around the 'special treatment' of colleagues with diagnosed ADHD – seemingly stigmatised for the benefits they received of extended deadlines, less pressured focus on work and more room for creatively pulling tasks together than other, undiagnosed employees were given. There was even a spiteful jealousy when it was brought up and the feeling that some people didn't believe it was a real disability. Despite this I had to bring it to my employer's attention. It felt as though the general opinion of the senior leadership team leaned towards notions of a personal flaw, such as laziness or incompetence, rather than recognising a medical neurological difference;

this lines up with undiagnosed young black women tagged as lazy or disobedient. 'She's hard to manage' comes to mind again here.

According to a study published in BMC Psychiatry, women with ADHD 'were more likely than their peers to have no or few qualifications, be in poorly paid employment, claim benefits, live in temporary or social housing and have a low income'.[6] Employers often lack awareness and understanding of ADHD, leading to its dismissal as a legitimate condition. Stereotypes and misconceptions about ADHD contribute to the dismissal of symptoms, such as impulsivity, distractibility and hyperactivity.

Do you have an official diagnosis?

Not yet, no.

Right, well, let me know what I can do to help.

That was the totality of the conversation. The insincere offer of 'help' that I wouldn't know where to start to describe or understand how to ask for. I felt brushed off. Dismissed. Like a child caught making excuses for late homework.

I didn't *know* what I needed. Those of us who have spent their entire lives in toxic self-dependence rarely know how to ask for help at the best of times. It had also been made apparent that I was not to speak to colleagues above my paygrade without going through my line manager, so I felt stuck. No human resource was in place at the time and I started to drown in the overwhelm of my circumstance. I felt like I had suddenly gone down in estimation for announcing I might have neurodivergence.

I was living in a sensory nightmare. The constant pinging of emails and endless meetings where I was expected to expunge my brain on the spot for creative solutions for departments that were out of my remit, on top of my own workload, made it impossible for me to focus, which led to anxiety. I knew the overwhelm was affecting my performance. I quickly fell into a depression. It felt like no one wanted to understand me.

There's a heavy narrative on what Team ADHD 'struggles' with. It's a lot, for sure. It has its challenges, but on the flipside: we're really good at failing and trying again, so we make great entrepreneurs, and we are ideas people – we know we can implement them, so we're confident and bold in our ideas. We are natural problem solvers, very curious about the world. We can find creative solutions that others can't see because of finely tuned pattern recognition. We demonstrate greater resilience and creativity, we can hyperfocus, we're good in a crisis, we have great conversational skills, we're spontaneous, we're entrepreneurial, we're empathetic and intuitive. We can think outside the box and we can see patterns where other people see chaos. We're courageous, we have the ability to find unique solutions to difficult problems, and we're able to think about different topics at once. We're high energy. Our willingness to take risks makes us pioneers and leaders.

I'm truly grateful that I got to find out about my condition through this employment. I've learned to ask people to judge me on my outcome, not my process. I need to work away from other people in a quiet room. I now know what I need in order to work productively. I need to work with my circadian rhythms. Over the last year I've tried and tested a multitude of holistic remedies to manage my ADHD since I hate big pharma and won't ingest that foul nonsense. It has in many ways enhanced my values around food and health sovereignty. Regular exercise, diet and variations of herbal remedies have all helped me negotiate coming back to myself and also manage my life-long low-key depression simultaneously.

Awareness of neurodivergence is on the rise as diagnosis increases. In an industry that is quick to call people lazy, disorganised or rude, I ask employers to consider what the underlying issues may be rather than assuming the worst. Your employees are your responsibility while they work for you. Make it your business to understand how they tick, what motivates them, what conditions make them thrive and what saps their soul and productivity. There may be an underlying factor that is affecting their performance or indeed *how* they perform their role. Regrettably, that's not always something I fully understood in earlier parts of my entrepreneurial and leadership journey. I'm sure I've made the same error in the past of misjudging people and not looking beyond the surface or taking a cynical or suspicious viewpoint. This experience was karma in a way. A lesson I needed to learn.

Historically, hospitality has always demanded speed and productivity from its workforce above all else. And honestly, not much has changed. As operation managers and hospitality employers we are often focused on the ever-disappearing bottom line. Those thin margins don't leave room for the meaty substantive work of unpacking the nuance around how a person shows up to work. If you can't get it done efficiently and within a well-worn set of standard procedures, well, there's a long line of other cooks or servers who can jump in at a moment's notice. I've been that boss. Hospitality staff are pretty dispensable on the front line. That's always been the case. It's why they have been treated so poorly for so long compared to office-based workers, who have reams of legislation supporting their rights to equal access and opportunity around not only fair pay but also disabilities – visible or otherwise. I don't think I've ever met a working chef who wasn't 'hyper' in some aspect of their work.

Employers, too, frequently fail to provide reasonable accommodations for individuals with ADHD, such as flexible work schedules, task organisation support or quiet workspaces. The dismissal of ADHD symptoms can result in increased stress, reduced productivity, and difficulty meeting expectations, leading to negative outcomes for employees – in my case, feeling isolated at work, anxious and depressed. Each day felt like being sucked dry of whatever usefulness could be drained from me in the limited hours each day I could be 'on' – I felt unseen for who I was and how I was trying to manage and what I was hoping to achieve. There was no room for creative problem solving in my own job role, yet I was often targeted for creative solutions to other department's problems.

ADHD is often underdiagnosed or misdiagnosed in women due to gender bias and differences in symptom presentation. Women with ADHD may exhibit predominantly inattentive symptoms, which are less visible and thus more likely to be overlooked or dismissed. Research shows that '14 per cent of girls with ADHD were prescribed antidepressants before being treated for ADHD compared to only 5 per cent of boys.'[7] On top of this, 'already subject to unique discrimination at the intersection of gender and race, Black girls with ADHD often remain undiagnosed because their symptoms are mischaracterized. Signs of inattentiveness or impulsivity, two main features of the disorder, could be mistaken for laziness or defiance.'[8]

Black and queer women with ADHD (hi, that's me) face additional challenges due to the intersectionality of gender, race and sexual orientation. Intersectional discrimination may exacerbate the dismissal of ADHD symptoms and limit access to resources or support. The dismissal of ADHD traits and symptoms in the workplace can have severe consequences for individuals, particularly women, and more specifically, black and queer women. It is crucial for employers to foster understanding, challenge stereotypes, and provide appropriate accommodations.

Additionally, incorporating a balanced diet and considering the potential benefits of certain foods and herbs can be helpful in managing ADHD symptoms. Some of those that I have found helpful have been highlighted throughout this essay. My diet has changed considerably since my diagnosis. A lot less red meat and meat in general – more pulses, grains, leaves and vegetables and tonnes of water every day. Hella herbs. Hydration has become everything to me in the last few years. I drink at least eight pints a day of spring water. We humans are like cucumbers, almost 90 per cent water – it's a vital intake for detoxifying our organs and blood as well as pulling through crucial life source energy. Everything is energy!

Increased variety of fruits and vegetables also helps – I consume a lot less salt, sugar and zero additives if I can help it. I have very little dairy or lactose – dairy milk is now a 'treat'. I eat a lot less cheese, which helps with clarity and focus and incidentally reduces congestion. I also eat less wheat and gluten products. I have nuts stashed to snack on throughout the day. Each morning with granola I eat walnuts (good for depression) and I find almonds especially powerful, though not everyone agrees. They combine these powerful elements of omega-3 fatty acids for brain and nervous system development, vitamin E antioxidants and the monounsaturated fats help slow age-related cognitive decline and improve memory. They also contain B vitamins for brain function including folate, thiamine and niacin, as well as magnesium which helps to relax muscles and reduce stress – overall good for brain function and memory.

My diet is always evolving to suit what my brain and body need in the moment and what the environment can provide sustainably. Despite being a chef for so many years I had fallen into terrible eating habits. Learning about ADHD helped me put myself back on the priority list, for not just my mental health but my diet, my emotional and spiritual health all at once. This diagnosis also dramatically changed my mindset about working with other people, helping me understand their limitations and allow space for their strengths.

So what's the recipe for supporting ADHD in the workplace? Support could look as simple as a mindful staff meal or canteen with offerings that support brain function. It could look like more regular rest breaks or more detailed task breakdowns. It could also look like allowing people to do what they're *best at* rather than forcing them to do tasks that clearly don't align with the way their brain functions. By addressing these issues, hospitality workplaces, both frontline in the kitchen and the offices behind, can become more inclusive and supportive for individuals with ADHD but also improve cognitive function and productivity generally among the team. In hospitality we focus a lot on what or how to deliver the best meal for the customer, but often we neglect what is the best meal for the team and its members.

Psychological Safety in Hospitality and Beyond

Hassel Aviles

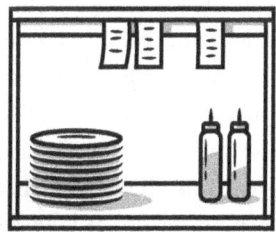

If you could redesign how restaurants operate, what would you change? Ooof, what a question! Truth is, I ask myself this often. What would I change? Dreaming up a different industry is one of my favourite pastimes. I love reimagining the hospitality sector. This passion stems from having spent the last two decades in and around the restaurant industry. I rarely felt safe and was always treated as disposable. There are various changes needed including adequate breaks, equitable and inclusive workplaces, leadership accountability, liveable wages and many more. Food service and hospitality demand an extraordinary amount of emotional labour that goes unrecognised and unpaid. The industry is built on various systems of oppression including tipping (which is a legacy of slavery), the brigade system (which designs kitchens in a strict hierarchy that often leads to abuse of power), inequity for marginalised identities and lack of diversity in leadership. Ideally I would implement all necessary changes, but my top choice would be to offer physical and psychological safety in the workplace for all hospitality and culinary professionals. The impact and benefits to both the business and the teams would have a positive ripple effect in a multitude of ways. Although restaurants are infamous for being unsafe workplaces, it really doesn't have to be this way and it's critical that we work towards systemic change in order to elevate the industry and, ultimately, save lives.

I've worked in hospitality for most of my life. I started in restaurants as a host over two decades ago and was quickly promoted to a server role. Following that I became a bartender and for years bounced around, working at over a dozen restaurants, bars, hotels and catering events. I was also an entrepreneur at one point; I co-owned a restaurant while running my own event production company. The entire time I worked in service, I lived with mental health challenges and used substances to cope. There was never any discussion of workplace mental health or psychological safety from owners or managers. I was never provided with mental health support in a workplace or access to resources, not once. Most places I worked in were toxic environments and I stayed for years because I internalised it all and, honestly, just didn't know better. I was young, unwell, hated myself, lacked self-worth and was unaware of employee rights. Even with all the abuse and exploitation that I witnessed and experienced, I survived. I gained resilience and years later have designed a full-time job where I get to advocate on behalf of the industry at large. Moving from shame to self-compassion is a long story to tell, especially since I had a lot of unlearning to do in both my personal life and career. Healing and recovery demanded I abandon harmful, archaic, oppressive ideas and replace them with more helpful principles of psychological safety and harm reduction. In order to stay alive, I have had to rewrite the narrative and do a lot of work to take my power back.

I have seen a lot of improvements over the years in restaurants and I also know that a lot hasn't changed from when I was a server. Two things can be true. Until we can face and acknowledge the systemic issues and spend time understanding how the industry got here, I don't believe we'll ever fully be able to move forward. We need to face the music, as they say. The work environment of restaurants and bars is a full sensory experience. My memories include a high volume of noise from music, yelling, equipment banging, pushing, shoving – it was constant, and always felt like a subtle way to normalise chaos. The lack of physical and emotional boundaries was exhausting and overwhelming. As a woman, I was also exposed to a barrage of sexual innuendos, and people rubbing up against me, including leaders, touching me without consent, even sniffing my hair or neck. This wasn't just by men – the first place I ever worked in when I was seventeen was actually owned and led by a woman. She let me know she was queer and always flirted with me. She also made endless inappropriate comments in front of tables of her guests, friends or partners. Initially I thought it was flattering, but after a while I started to feel very uncomfortable. Regardless of how I felt, I was never allowed to question anything and instead always had my inexperience held against me. She'd say, 'You don't get it, this is just how it is. You'll understand when you're older and have worked in restaurants longer.'

Now, decades later, I understand that statements like this are used to emotionally manipulate and exploit people. Disorganisation, lack of good infrastructure and workplace regulations have ultimately enabled an abuse of power that is often used to take advantage of the most vulnerable.

Alcohol and other substances are used to mask what is actually happening too. Although substance use is a coping mechanism, it is harmful and is often used as a tool of manipulation to force bonds or a false sense of community. It is common for binge drinking and partying to be sold as 'the culture', normalised as camaraderie or even forced on new team members as a form of hazing. In cases of despair or pain, substances are often offered as a solution. The entire time I worked in restaurants and bars, I was living with mental illness in the form of depression, social anxiety and trauma. Instead of being met with compassion, I was constantly told to 'check my shit at the door', as if it was possible to divorce myself from my humanity. Instead of open dialogue, support and resources for workplace mental health, there was stigma, shame, yelling and punishment. It was dehumanising. Although I was mostly surrounded by people who were also struggling, no one addressed it openly or directly in the workplace. There was an intolerance for any and all emotional experiences except for anger. Instead of leadership signposting me towards helpful resources, substances were encouraged and often provided as a way to cope. This included having managers offer me numerous shots and other drugs during my shift and the reminder that there were beers in the walk-in fridge available. If service was going well, we celebrated by drinking – and if things were not going well, we were told drinking takes the edge off. Either way, 'Have a drink!' quickly created a dependency habit. After hours, the doors were locked and very often the drinking and partying continued until sunrise. The lines were blurred between work and personal life, between professional relationships and intimate ones and between what I was comfortable with and what was being forced on me. There was an unspoken casual nature about substance use in the hospitality community that made it easy to normalise violating people and for employers to neglect their responsibilities.

The traditional restaurant business model is antiquated and it's clear that the industry needs a software upgrade. Employers have been neglecting their responsibility to provide physical and psychological safety for their employees, resulting in an abundance of toxic work environments. As a result, restaurants, bars and hotels haemorrhage money to turnover costs at an average rate of $4,129 per hire,[1] and experience labour challenges, with 62 per cent of operators saying they can't staff up to meet demand, and 80 per cent saying they have a hard time filling open positions.[2] This means most establishments remain stuck with low profit margins, with the average restaurant falling between 3–5 per cent.[3] This is all interconnected. It's clear the industry needs help!

Industry leaders have the most power, privilege and influence in the workplace yet most managers don't know how to foster psychological safety and many operators don't even know what the term means. Many leadership skills required to manage workplace mental health in restaurants, bars or hotels have not been traditionally taught in hospitality or culinary schools. As a result, owners, operators and executive chefs who make business decisions that impact the workplace are misinformed, unequipped for the demands of the job and respond with reactive solutions instead of implementing proactive prevention tactics. This has a big impact. A global study from the Workforce Institute found that employee mental health is impacted more by managers than doctors or therapists, and even the same as the employee's spouse or partner.[4]

There is a massive need for systemic change to incorporate workplace mental health education so that leaders can make a positive impact by offering access to and promoting mental health resources and fostering open communication about workplace mental health. Many hospitality and culinary workers who criticise the industry often say the biggest issue in restaurants is inadequate pay, low hourly rates and wage theft. There is no question that we need to address wage theft and ensure that all workers are adequately compensated. This needs to change immediately, but even with that, research by MIT Sloan has shown that a toxic work environment and culture is ten times more powerful than compensation in predicting a company's attrition rate and employee turnover.[5] These issues are so rampant and normalised that many say it is 'simply a cost of doing business.' This is false, it is short-sighted and demonstrates poor business skills.

Psychological safety has many benefits, including increasing employee retention, creativity, collaboration, innovation and even results in a hefty financial return on investment. Investing in workplace mental health has an ROI that has been documented in various sectors. Every dollar spent on workplace mental health and support for teams is an investment in the business, not an expense. A World Economic Forum study shows that employers supporting workplace mental health see a return of $4 for every $1 invested.[6] It turns out that creating a psychologically safe work environment is the gift that keeps on giving. Not only does it help manage labour issues, workplace culture and employee engagement, but when Google did research to find what makes a 'perfect team' they discovered the most important factor for high performance, productivity and effectiveness is psychological safety.[7]

In 2018, I chose to challenge the status quo and make a career change, intersecting my food-service background with my mental health lived experience, and helped launch Not 9 to 5. As a Canadian incorporated nonprofit we have headquarters in Toronto, Ontario with partners and impact worldwide. The work we do was founded on instinct and is now cemented in data. Our humble beginnings as a local grassroots initiative quickly grew us into a nonprofit global leader in mental health advocacy and education for the hospitality sector, with partners in Canada, the US, the UK and beyond. These days, as the executive director of Not 9 to 5, I primarily focus on practical education about psychological safety. This workplace term was coined by Harvard Business School professor Amy Edmondson, PhD, and my preferred definition for psychological safety is: *An environment where people feel it is safe to show up as their authentic self, make mistakes, be vulnerable with each other, give and receive feedback and take risks without any fear of negative consequences to how they'll be perceived or for their job itself.*

The term 'mental health' is rarely understood as a neutral term. Even with growing global awareness, it is still stigmatised and mostly associated with negative experiences. As a kid, I always heard it described as something to feel ashamed of. As a teen, mental health was talked about as a 'problem to solve' and when I entered the workforce, conversations about it were avoided at all costs. Stigma causes people to suffer in silence. Toxic work culture feeds stigma and shame around mental health and substance use challenges; this in turn prevents folks from seeking and accepting help when needed.[8] Everyone has mental health as an aspect of our overall health, similar to physical health. Our mental well-being is fluid and can fluctuate from stable to unstable and vice versa. Yet in restaurants, there is an avoidance of investment in workplace mental health and a deep denial of facts, even with a rise in mental health crises, substance use challenges and suicide.[9]

Access to basic mental health education and training can prevent shame and self-blame. I felt shame about my depression, anxiety and trauma, and as a result I didn't feel worthy of care. I internalised my experiences and feelings as a personal failure. I thought that the 'peak and valley' fluctuations and imbalance were an indication of weakness or unworthiness. I hid my symptoms as much as possible and overcompensated by prioritising my physical appearance, smiling and being social more than I desired. Now I am a recovering people-pleaser because I understand what I felt was a natural reaction to my life, events and environments. Stigma prevented me and many others from speaking out and left me unaware that many people around me were having similar experiences and feelings. I didn't know how to identify my own symptoms, lacked adaptive coping skills and had no tools to regulate my nervous system.

Intersectionality plays into all of this as well. My life and identities have been woven around mental illness, substance dependency, racism, white supremacy, misogyny, patriarchy, queerness, sexism, violence, childhood trauma, oppression and feminism, just to name a few. When I was younger the cultural norms of my family and Latin culture taught me to neglect my mental health. My ancestral roots are in Chile in South America, with ties to the Mapuche Indigenous Peoples from both of my parents. They emigrated to Toronto, Canada before I was born, and my first language was Spanish. I didn't learn English until I entered the school system at four years old. I was raised in a loving home with parents who always cared for me. My family is incredible, and yet what I learned about mental health from the adults in my life was linked to shame, confusion, silence and secrecy. It was not one or the other – life experiences are not binary. I do love my family, and I can acknowledge that some of their actions caused me harm. I also appreciate that they did the best they could with what they had; they were also raised to stay silent about mental health.

Even in a loving home, I experienced various forms of trauma in my childhood. It wasn't until I was in my mid-twenties that I would gain the vocabulary to express my emotions, describe my mental health or understand what intergenerational trauma is. It took me another decade before I reflected on how I sought out similar dynamics from my family in a different environment of chaos: restaurants. Chilean culture is similar to many other Latin countries, passionate, expressive, loud and outwardly caring. We are deeply impacted by various forms of oppression and centuries of colonialism. My memories of family functions include an environment centred around food and drink, a festive mood, an overwhelming sensory experience of loud music, people yelling over each other, lack of physical boundaries, events that lasted late into the night and absolutely no one ever discussing mental health. As a highly sensitive person who experiences social anxiety, these parties felt like an attack on my mental well-being. Even when I tried to speak up for myself, the hierarchy of power resided with adults and I was repeatedly told to know my place. It was expected that I would suppress my needs, voice and emotions. I have many memories I cherish that brought me joy in these environments, but they were moments. I learned how to adapt, assimilate and neglect my mind and intuition. I then carried these maladaptive coping tools with me into restaurant work.

When I first started working in hospitality, restaurants felt familiar to me. Many of the traits and descriptions outlined above from my childhood were similar in restaurants, kitchens and bars. I was already well versed in various harmful and toxic mentalities that were accepted industry wide. Although many of these norms are harmful and toxic, they are still implemented and adopted. Managers and leaders will train you to be 'strong' by avoiding vulnerability and discouraging boundaries. Ableism and misogyny are felt in every corner. Various forms of abuse are normalised and there is a lack of leadership accountability. Questioning power structures and involving team input are discouraged. There's emotional manipulation in being told 'we're a family', gaslighting and dismissing people's complaints. Part of why this continues is due to the fact that oppressive systems are built into the foundation of the hospitality service industry with organisational and operational norms like tipping and the brigade system. The influence of the brigade system creates a work environment that leaves little room for humanity, emotions and the spectrum of mental health experiences. This rigid military-style influence creates workplaces that lead to exploitation and in the name of 'efficiency' leaves little to no room for adequate nourishment, rest, pay, safety or support. The constant pressure to follow the chain of command at whatever cost disconnects workers from themselves and leaves them at the mercy of the leader's orders. The influences of the brigade system have seeped out of the kitchen and spread like a virus across the industry. I remember as a bartender and server I was expected to follow the lead of my manager, and if they didn't take breaks, neither did I. The only exception seemed to be leaving for a cigarette.

This structure needs to be challenged and redesigned in order to reflect all of the people that make up the workforce. An antidote to all of this is psychological safety. It pushes back on the mentality of sacrificing your mental and physical health for the job. We need to abolish the idea of seeing vulnerability as a weakness. We need to stop demanding staff repress and suppress any and all emotional experiences. This absurd concept is dehumanising and is as harmful to the business as it is to people. It's time to acknowledge the harm caused and retire the outdated practices that don't serve us. And we have to invest in mental health education, training, support and resources across the industry. This also includes developing leadership skills and leaning into the discomfort of change.

Gaining mental health education and language for understanding emotional experiences helps people learn new ways to navigate and cope. It helps to shed judgement and replace it with support skills by adopting more appropriate vocabulary and learning how to identify, understand and respond to common symptoms. With support skills, we begin to understand how to help people feel less alone in a time of need. It is important to acknowledge that we can offer support for mental health just like we do with first aid and physical health. When someone cuts their hand, as a manager you are not expected to stitch that person up. Instead, with their consent, you connect them with a more appropriate medical professional. It can be the same for mental health. When someone is struggling or seeking support, we can practise active listening skills and offer to refer them to a professional or other support of their choice.

We can gain more by using empathy and compassion, centring humanity, treating everyone with dignity and respect as well as being direct in our communication. When we practise active listening skills it can change our relationships and lives. We all play a role in unlearning the toxic mentalities that keep us oppressed. We will never find liberation or healing in work environments that don't recognise our humanity. This is all very complex and nuanced, but one step at a time we have begun to see change. Baby steps saved my life. People sometimes say that it's helpful to live your life one day at a time. In my experience, some days can only be survived by focusing on one breath at a time. The hospitality and restaurant industry can adapt to learn more about psychological safety and create a work environment where people feel supported, seen, heard and held. After seeing so much change in the last few years, I have never felt more hopeful that the past does not define the future of restaurants. We are in an era of expanding our understanding of what we have known the industry to be and have increased access to concrete evidence of the power of psychological safety in the workplace. Other industries have been implementing these vital changes in the workplace; it's time for restaurants to do the same.

I Am Not Safe If My Whole Self Is Not Safe

Vanessa Parish

I began my career as a chef with the goal of creating a legacy that honours my ancestors and champions the community. The same people that for hundreds of years were reduced to involuntary service in kitchens. Now their descendants are fighting to be allowed back into what we created. Being an Indigenous Black Queer woman has never been easy, but I have always been dedicated to contributing value for the betterment of my people. I think about where I was working and living when I was younger. I would ask myself, 'Do you feel safe here?' I did have a group of folks that accepted my racial diversity, but I didn't have a space where I could live authentically as a Queer woman. I retained the lesson that even in the face of adversity, my food and passion had to curate something instrumental and impactful. I had to find my own place.

As I worked my way through life and continued learning about my culinary craft, I found many places I could call home. There were people that supported me and offered their knowledge for my growth. I would be able to go to the grocer and meet with the butcher about my next dish. I would get educated on what to look for in the freshest ingredients. The local hang-out spot would always be the place where I could find my friends and break bread with them. Growing up in the South taught me that the community can also be your family. My grandmother's kitchen is a hearth and the neighbourhood served as a nurturing space. During the summer, the entire street would gather together for cookouts, everyone bringing their own dish. This is where I learned what safe spaces truly meant. There is a feeling of being cared for, watched over and encouraged. However, the constant question at the back of my mind would still appear. *Will I ever be able to live out as myself completely?* I recognised that there would still be times where my safe spaces differed depending on where I was and how I presented myself.

As time went on, the comfort I felt began to change. When I officially entered the culinary world in a professional capacity, I was reminded that I was the minority. I started as a pastry chef in the South, which is notorious for its prejudices. Whether it be because of my Queerness, gender identity, race, or a mixture of them all, my existence was challenged and ease was taken away from me. I was only offered windows of opportunity in predominantly white-led kitchens. In these kitchens, I would experience awkwardness and blatant discrimination. This led to a series of shut doors and work offers that I was overqualified to accept. 'I don't hire Blacks.' 'You're too pretty to be on my line, you'll distract my boys.' 'No, I'm not going to grab that pallet of flour for you. Get one of your boyish girlfriends to do it for you.' I was always out of place. The feeling of being an outcast shadowed me not only in the kitchen but in common world spaces as well. My neighbourhoods of safety were beginning to shift.

And then my neighbourhood began to change, and this shift came in the form of gentrification. It is a catalyst for the destruction of the community, and we are told that it is 'good for us'. Gentrification is sold as a positive action that creates growth for a barren population. This new form of modern colonisation has been perpetuated these past decades all throughout the United States. Now the last land of Brown generational wealth has been given a price that they couldn't refuse or risk being pushed out anyways. The local grocer next door has become an avant-garde coffee shop. I am in a new space, but it is not new territory. The foundation that our neighbourhood was built on is beginning to be bulldozed into condominiums.

And yet I started to feel conflicted with this era of new age colonialism. My intersections began to have some contradictions. That same avant-garde shop has a rainbow flag in the window. As a Queer person, this is the first time I have been able to publicly see something like that in this area. The newer restaurants started to hire a diverse staff and prioritise health over wealth. The systemic oppression that we fight for was being recognised as an actual problem. Being in communal spaces where Queer people are welcome was a new experience. However, are these spaces actually made for me? A Brown Queer person?

The culinary experience is not immune to this contradiction. This example reflects that just because I exist in a marginalised space, I am not absolved of privilege. As a culinarian, it is exciting to see new restaurants and concepts appear. But didn't that restaurant arrive because the shopping centre that housed local eateries was torn down? What do you do when you are used to being the only one not heard or appreciated, and then the opportunity for that to change arrives? What happens when one part of your intersection gets a chance to thrive but could be at the expense of another marginalised intersection you belong to? This kind of erasure breeds more ignorance as the new community won't recognise the hands that have nourished this neighbourhood.

This also raises a question about the split of growth and access versus the oppression of the community. My grandmother's oldest friend is elderly and owns acres of farmland in rural North Carolina. This land is in a prime area of the highway that could be used to attract travellers. Her farmland produces 60 per cent of the crops needed to feed the nearby towns. The buyers have already bought the land around her, which could squeeze her out anyway due to the construction potentially damaging her land.

Gentrification has proven that the goal is more about wealth and acquisition than it is about the community and the improvements it is supposed to benefit from. Gentrification cannot win me over with its innocent facade. From the outside it is considered diverse progress and taken with pride, but it utilises this concept to contribute to harmful practices.

I continue to be committed to ensuring that all of my intersecting identities are secure and included. I have realised that I am not safe if my whole self is not safe. When you separate identities, you separate the connection to each community. The nuances of gentrification contribute to this separation. I have to protect that Indigenous Black Queer girl that has held on to finding her new home. I want to be able to celebrate a new Queer space without knowing that it came at the cost of my other community being unhoused and misplaced. I want to contribute to solving this problem of disequilibrium, the celebration of Queer progress while dealing with the erasure of racially marginalised culture, by utilising my superpower. By being unapologetically myself, and existing as a thriving and diverse individual, I can show up in places I wouldn't otherwise have been considered part of. I'm grateful that I get to showcase the best parts of myself and to have been given the freedom to use my skill set in these environments.

I became a leader in my career and have dedicated myself to creating a work environment that I would've dreamed of having while I was coming of age in my culinary journey. I started advocating for paid time off, lunch breaks, shorter holiday blackout periods, higher wages and completely equitable job opportunities. I wanted my team members who were facing hardship, experiencing mental health issues or who had disabilities to know that this was a kitchen where they did not have to suppress those experiences in order to retain employment. I wanted to take advantage of the chance at having the smallest upper hand and use it to elevate my folx.

When I founded my catering business, I was dedicated to finding Queer Brown women who wanted a chance to learn and lead. I networked with others in the business to establish connections. I co-founded an organisation dedicated to building safer communities, contributing solutions for food inequity and unethical practices for Queer folx. For me, this highlights that no matter where we are, it's the people who create the home. My future is nurturing the purpose I found in the culinary world. I grew up to provide a safe space for the others around me.

Hamantaschen

Abigail Koffler

Growing up, hamantaschen were a source of joy – part of one of the first holidays of the year, a wintery sprinkle of sugar and fun. Traditional fillings were things like prune and poppy seed, but I grew up filling them with chocolate and sprinkles and peanut butter chips and Nutella. I've always loved baking them with my family; we use an oil-based sugar cookie dough recipe from a kosher cookbook (we've never kept kosher but tradition's tradition). The dough chills overnight (my mom does the lion's share of work here, making multiple batches in the KitchenAid mixer she got as a wedding present), and then it's go time.

In February 2021, shortly before Purim, the holiday that calls for hamantaschen, I woke up one morning to a text from a friend, sent late the night before. 'Are you OK? Have you read it?' As I read the text, my heart started racing. I sat up in bed, unable to put my phone down. I had no idea what she was talking about.

After trawling through Google for over an hour, I found the object of her concerns, an article that mentioned me and my beliefs about Jewish food in a very negative light. I had no idea this was coming and braced myself for the worst. Dealing with internet trolls could be seen as a price to pay for using the internet. I disagree with that: no one should have to face the unwarranted vitriol of strangers online.

I've been online for a long time – I remember joining Twitter in 2010, at the age of sixteen, inspired by a cool camp counsellor who used the platform. My early tweets were about the food options at camp – the day we walked to a local ice cream parlour was a thrill. In 2017, I started This Needs Hot Sauce, a food newsletter and community. It's read by thousands of people around the world and I share details about my family, friends, travels. I've shared stories about Covid, moving, deaths in my family, money and more. It's pretty personal and I choose to share a lot more about myself than the average person on the internet, which also helps my career. And I was still blown away by the experience of receiving such negative attention with no warning. It happened overnight, truly. It was scary and hard to explain. It felt like a flow of notifications I couldn't keep up with, like a moving sidewalk carrying me somewhere I didn't know was safe and I hadn't even planned to go.

At the time, I spent my afternoons teaching kids at a Manhattan synagogue, which was a great excuse to spend a few hours off my phone, even though I was very distracted (gotta set a good example). Working on stories for freelance assignments was hard – it gave me too much unadulterated time to refresh my notifications.

My mentions got ugly. My friend who works in breaking news and had experience covering Trump rallies and mass shootings confessed she had been monitoring things and searching for my name to make sure nothing weird was happening – I was grateful and privileged to have someone with experience in this area in my corner. Her newsroom had a security team to help their employees if things got ugly, but freelancers have no such protections. I was lucky in the end – I got a lot of opinions, from Jews and non-Jews, a few anti-Semitic people in my mentions who were quickly blocked, and the whole thing blew over in a few weeks.

What inspired all this conversation? A cookie, of all things. And not just any cookie, but hamantaschen: a triangular cookie eaten to celebrate the Jewish holiday of Purim, which falls in February or March of the Gregorian calendar. It's sometimes compared to Halloween because observing it means re-enacting the story in costume. You're also encouraged to get so drunk you lose your senses in celebration (on my college campus, this meant *lots* of parties).

The cookies originated in Europe in the 1500s. The word comes from German, and the shape symbolises either Haman's ears, pockets or hat. The original filling was poppy seed, which some people think is a reference to Purim hero Esther's diet. In the story of Purim, found in the Book of Esther, the eponymous heroine saves the Jewish people from a villain named Haman who seeks to arrange their demise. Esther hides her identity to marry the king, hears of Haman's dangerous plot to hang Jews on the gallows, and then reveals the truth and saves the Jewish people. It's a story that resonates with many Jews, from young girls excited about a female hero to adults contemplating rising anti-Semitism around the world.

I love the symbolism of eating a cookie to chip away at a villain who was plotting the extermination of the Jewish people. When we tell the Purim story, it's traditional to boo or use noisemakers to drown out Haman's name. Our survival is louder than those that tried to end us, a theme of many Jewish holidays. Truly, what's not to like about this holiday and its food?

The kitchen at my parents' house becomes a production line with bags of flour, bread boards, and silver bowls stacked with fillings distributed across the table and countertops. Everyone grabs an apron and passes rolling pins back and forth. We use cookie cutters to create round bases, dollop filling in the centre and seal the triangle with a squeeze (a drop of water is available but usually not necessary). My parents have two ovens in their kitchen and when we make these cookies, both are on full blast and working hard. All the cooling racks are out. It's a constant rotation from the floured table to the cookie sheet to the rack. A few cookies accidentally burn, a few open in the oven, but the yield is high and we've gotten a lot faster as adults. One of the most beautiful parts of celebrating Purim is creating gift bags called Shalach Manot for neighbours. As a kid I would walk up and down the street in Kew Gardens, New York, ringing their doorbells and leaving boxes for neighbours. Now, I like to bring bags to friends and the free fridge in my neighbourhood.

As an adult who lives 6.5 miles from her parents, I've gotten to continue this hamantaschen-making tradition into my thirties. I still invite friends and so does my sister. We experiment with new fillings like cheesecake from beloved food blogger and cookbook author Deb Perelman. Breads Bakery in Manhattan is even making savoury hamantaschen inspired by pizza; I haven't tried that yet. We add sprinkles to the dough and make slightly less of a mess than we did as kids. In 2018 I started teaching at a Hebrew school in Manhattan and I had the honour of making hamantaschen with the kids, in person before Covid and then on Zoom. It was so rewarding to pass on the tradition because my most positive memories of Jewish holidays all centre around food.

If these cookies sound relatively harmless, you're right; but what I learned through my brush with internet trolls is that they're actually kind of hated. My tweet came from an attempt to find recipes for a class I was teaching and became a fight over woke culture. It showed people will draw wild conclusions from just about anything, if someone powerful fans the flame. People dug up old Instagram photos and called my homemade cookies dry and not homemade, others said I was stopping innovation and promoting colonialist thinking by wanting to continue traditions and share family recipes. I was too politically correct, too woke, too irrelevant. One person made a very crude joke about the cookie's shape, another made a cruel comment about my face, and others said the only Jewish dessert that was really good was cheesecake (which we actually do eat on a different holiday). Each troll was angry about a slightly different thing and felt it was their duty to tell me about it, right away . . .

Some uninspired bakery hamantaschen and childhood memories clearly gave the cookies a bad reputation – people shared stories of temple basements and stale pastries. I would never claim it's impossible to make bad hamantaschen – they exist. Poppy seed doesn't have the cultural cachet of challah French toast or chocolate babka. I get it, we've all been to an event with some bad catering, but I defended something I've loved since childhood and was told it was stupid to care.

I've seen Jewish food go through many phases in my lifetime – certain dishes are trendy (rainbow bagels anyone?) and certain dishes get forgotten. I'm still waiting for mandelbrot, a Jewish cookie that's baked twice (similar to biscotti), to get their due. My grandma's recipe with dried cherries and pistachios is incredible. Israeli food has become very popular in the United States, with restaurants like Zahav in Philadelphia leading the way. But I'm not Israeli and the Ashkenazi food of Jews from Eastern Europe, which is where my family's traditional recipes come from, is very different – and less trendy. As with many cultures that are not part of the American food media mainstream (which is very white and Christian), versions of Jewish foods can make their way to the spotlight, changing along the way. Change isn't a bad thing, and these dishes have certainly evolved through pogroms, migrations, wars and alterations to the food system (Crisco was not in historical recipes, but it's in many Kosher cookbooks). I get annoyed when Jewish food has to be food porny to get attention. I like latkes with sour cream for Hanukkah, rather than in a breakfast sandwich, but it's also cool to see latkes become more recognised.

One of the things that most appeals to me about Judaism is the culture of discourse. Debate and argument are woven deep in the fabric of our society – studying, talking through things and disagreeing are acts of worship. The saying 'two Jews, three opinions' rings true whether the Jews in question are ten or eighty years old (our holiday meals get loud).

Rather than push consensus, our tradition is one of arguments and discussion about how to do things and what's actually right (or if there is a right answer, which there isn't always). But this discourse is harder to have online; the way we treat people who share pieces of themselves on the internet is broken, particularly if those people share things that run counter to mainstream culture. At the same time, I'm grateful the internet exists – it's given me a window to learn and connect with people and stories I wouldn't have known about otherwise. I also love memes and the laughter they bring to my day via group chats.

Arguing about a hamantaschen recipe continues a throughline of thousands of years of conversation and celebration. It connects me to events from my own family, like the time my grandfather got fired from his job as a radio show host in college for using his real last name when signing off. He was supposed to use a fake one that didn't sound so Jewish. My grandparents later started one of the first synagogues in Orange County, California, which I last visited for a celebration of his life in early 2023. I love hearing their stories of growing up near Philadelphia, where the grown-ups spoke Yiddish when they didn't want the kids to understand. Those are the stories I want to pass on to my future family, along with lots of recipes. I'll probably post pictures too – let the comments roll.

Author's note: When I think about the Judaism I grew up with and want to pass down, it means speaking up against injustice and genocide, no matter who is being targeted. Never again means now, and I stand with the people of Palestine and others facing oppression.

Was Anthony Bourdain Wrong About Vegan Food?

Lee Tran Lam

My grandmother was the first vegetarian I knew. I can't retrace any conversation we ever had on the subject, but I can mentally zoom in on dishes from her dinner table in Sydney, Australia, in high-definition detail – even thirty years later.

There was the doona-scramble of fried eggs, pan-hot with bitter melon crescents and seasoned with a dusty hurricane of black pepper (our family used the pre-ground supermarket stuff that softly trailed out of cheap shakers – freshly cracked pepper would be a ritzy discovery I'd make much later in life). I remember the stacked steamers that held bowls of wobbly tofu pudding – finished with a sweetened drizzle of bracing ginger syrup. I even had a fondness for the way she'd make me two-minute noodles before school – she'd sink the dried noodle cake into a bowl, submerge it with hot water and place a plate on top to seal in the steam. The noodle strands would gradually soften and unnest and this lazy heat-trap would leave the wheaty ringlets surrounded by a yellow border of grease, which I adored.

I was astonished to learn, decades later, that there is a 'correct' way for grandmothers to prepare two-minute noodles – well, in Hong Kong, anyway, where Tea Craft's Arthur Tong is from. The Sydney-based tea seller explained the 'gor lang mo' method to me. In Cantonese, it translates as 'passing through a cold stream': you're meant to strain the noodles multiple times, until that incriminating yellow grease ring is erased from the bowl. To be honest, I preferred my grandmother's approach and the way the oily haloes would circle the broth, like the rings used by lifeguards.

My grandmother had lived several lives before I knew her – she was mother to ten children and experienced the fallout of the Vietnam War; her roots were Chinese and she'd ended up in Australia. But none of this backstory was overtly clear to me as a kid. There was a haze around her history and my school-aged observation skills were – to be honest – best optimised for cartoon-hopping between TV channels, not deep explorations of her vivid migrant backstory. My childhood memories of her could actually be replayed like a hypnotic soundtrack: the low, insistent tempo of her prayers at the Buddhist shrines in our home, repeated and whispered, and the way she'd hit a small gong at key moments, its chime ringing out to compete with the Saturday morning kids' shows I attempted to watch at the same time.

When she wasn't praying, she was gentle and reserved: she'd place cut apple pieces into bowls of water. The bare, angular shapes would bathe and soften, before she eventually dipped them out and savoured them once a meal had finished – each bite mellowed by that cleansing bowl-soak.

You couldn't unlink my grandmother's identity as a vegetarian from the fact she was a Buddhist. The two distinguishing details were forever locked together and impossible to separate; avoiding harm with each bowl, stir-fry and chopstick-jostle made sense to me. Growing up in a Buddhist household, guilt over killing animals was incredibly hard to shake. It was genuinely traumatising if I came across a cockroach – I still remember how my cousin and I intensely cried after we killed one in my teenage bedroom; we didn't exactly want to co-exist with the pests, but were overwhelmed by the idea of snuffing out the life force of something. My dad loved to fish and I was truly upset by my certainty that he'd be reincarnated as a sea creature one day, his mouth inevitably torn by an angler's hook.

This was how my kid brain operated.

Maybe this line of thinking primed me to become a vegetarian when I was sixteen. I had an email friend that I'd met from a fan-run mailing list for the band Weezer and they once sent a message that described, in such hyper-graphic detail, the ways farmed animals were treated. I ended up so revolted, I couldn't imagine stomaching meat again.

I started my vegetarian diet by eating sticky rice my mother had left around and ended up dousing vegetables in Chicken Tonight sauce during my earliest rookie attempts to 'cook'. My meals gradually got less tragic from this point.

Initially, my mother was annoyed about my dietary switch and the dinner-prep complications it involved – but then I overheard her bragging to her friends that I'd turned vegetarian and she happily banked all the Buddhist cred that came with that revelation. That said, my parents often took me to seafood restaurants for my birthday: they enjoyed tank-fresh dishes, while I struggled with steamed greens (the only vegetarian-friendly dish on the menu).

But zoom out beyond this one moment and I would eventually experience so much more than side dishes of saintly greens. Becoming vegetarian actually introduced me to a dizzying spectrum of flavours and cuisines – I'm convinced I still would be on a 'Devon meat on white bread with tomato sauce' thrill-free diet if I hadn't said no to meat. Places often have one 'vego' option available if you eat out, so you have to try whatever it is, because the alternative is an unappetising stint of starvation. This scenario has created a treasury of first-time experiences and culinary introductions that I've since become grateful for, from that first falafel roll bite to the ume-tart (plum-tart) punch of onigiri and braised hibiscus flowers, cooked al pastor style and served with pineapple jam on sopes.

When I drop by Walid El Sabbagh's Koshari Korner eatery, I order the signature koshari: a fantastic jumble of spiced tomato sauce, fried onion flakes, chickpeas, lentils, rice and pasta splashed with garlic vinegar. His venue specialises in Egyptian street food and the star item – koshari – happens to be the nation's signature dish. He explains to me that many staples are naturally vegan in Egypt because meat is an extravagance. Before arriving in Australia he was a marine engineer, but without local experience he was unable to continue his trade in Sydney. The recipes of his grandmother back in Alexandria created a lifeline for him here and he launched Koshari Korner first as a market stall at an Eid event, before eventually expanding it to a permanent eatery in Marrickville, New South Wales.

Tyree Barnette runs his Southern Soul market stall with his wife Tracina: their barbecue jackfruit ribs, collard greens and cornbread tell a story about the cuisine of his African American ancestors and the dishes of resilience created from scraps they were allocated while cruelly enslaved. Barnette likes to highlight the connection between Southern Soul's vegan menu and the plant-based roots of West African cuisine – as well as memories of his American grandparents dunking cornbread into collard green juices, while golden crumbs cascaded down his own shirt as he consumed the cornbread. I'm grateful he shared his story with me for inclusion in the first *New Voices on Food* book, one of the projects I launched with my Diversity In Food Media collective in Australia. It was also an important story that, up until this point, wasn't heard much, and it – like his business – was partly a reaction to seeing fried chicken joints proliferate as a hot food trend in Sydney, without much cultural context about their African American roots.

One of the mainstays of Newtown's King Street used to be Khamsa – a plant-based Palestinian venue that was also the city's only Palestinian cafe. Here, the owner Sarah Shaweesh cooked musakhan with oyster mushrooms in place of the traditional sumac-spiced chicken, and presented her version of cheesy knafeh, a dessert from her mother's city of Nablus. Through her menu, she reminded people of the existence of Palestine, a country her grandfather was forcibly removed from in 1948.

Head back to King Street today and you'll find a truly diverse line-up of vegan eateries:

- Golden Lotus, which offers Vietnamese dishes like claypot eggplant, 'duck' bamboo noodle soups and drumsticks hit with makrut lime and chilli.
- Vandal, where tacos are topped with Peruvian yellow chilli katsu, Korean-style eggplant, and salt and pepper oyster mushrooms dressed with a smoked chilli and agave vinaigrette.
- Gigi Pizzeria, which survived the hysteria surrounding owner Marco Matino's decision to go vegan in 2015: it retained its Associazione Verace Pizza Napoletana certification and reminded people that cheese-free pizza could be legitimately delicious and, in fact, the classic marinara is as traditional – and as vegan – as any pizza can be.
- I Should Be Souvlaki, which is the outcome of Emma Langley surprising her partner Adam Papastathopoulos with a plant-based version of souvlaki so convincing that he was immediately transported back to his grandmother's table. Their marinated-cauliflower souvlaki wrap, served 'Santorini style' (stuffed with hot chips), is a salty, garlicky, dill-rich knockout.
- La Petite Fauxmagerie, a vegan cheese shop that sells plant-based blue cheese that wowed a cheese judge, and house-made garlic feta and butter that is genuinely great. Co-owner Michelle van Rensburg credits her politician parents – who fought against apartheid in South Africa – as inspiring her ethical stance.
- Le Gourmand, a French deli specialising in vegan macarons, croissants and foie gras. It's run by Frédéric Mariage, who used to be an écailler (seafood chef)

back in France, and now contemplates how to make dairy-free crème brûlée.

My favourite vegan spot on this street might be Comeco Foods, which is run by Yu Ozone. It could also qualify as the most inclusive cafe in the city. It's shaped by her food allergies and intolerances, so everything – from the Japanese falafel to the onigiri, curry and smoky barbecue miso sushi rolls – is gluten-free and vegan. Her sourdough doughnuts – flavoured with matcha custard, organic cinnamon sugar, spiced apples or sweet adzuki bean paste – were first made for a friend's son who was severely allergic to gluten, nuts, seeds, egg and dairy.

Imagine trying to bake something delicious with those sharp limitations.

Ozone's Japanese doughnuts – fashioned from organic brown rice dough that's been left to ferment for days – have been such a success that they've caused people to cry, particularly one woman who was unable to eat conventional doughnuts for twenty years and assumed she'd been forever cut off from that joyful, sugar-sprinkled experience. Ozone also flew to Japan to learn how to produce gluten-free rice bread – and later revised the recipe over a hundred times to get it right – and now creates these charming pizza breads (or cheese and corn mayo equivalents) that taste like being in Tokyo. Her team grinds their organic brown rice flour in the cafe to avoid possible contamination and to assure allergy-conscious diners, and Comeco Foods produces its own gluten-free and vegan tempura flour.

I once enthusiastically told some podcast hosts about the lengths Ozone has gone to for her menu and they were shocked that she wasn't more well known. I can't help but wonder how different her profile would be if she was a dude chef who'd undergone Michelin-starred training in Europe – maybe people would be bragging about her custom-ground rice flour, or the fact she spent six years masterminding her tempura batter which is miraculously free of egg and wheat. But because she's drawing on her Japanese grandmother's cooking knowledge about traditional fermented foods (like amazake and miso) or opting for the kasaneni method of tightly layering vegetables in a pot to maximise their flavours (instead of some theatrical, high-wattage approach), are her efforts getting unfairly overlooked?

Besides ten-course family wedding banquets, I can't recall my grandmother dining out much before she passed away and I wonder what she would have made of these eateries. Perhaps she would have preferred her plainly sliced and rinsed apples. Growing up with her Buddhist approach to cooking made me appreciate that food isn't always about the punchiest, loudest flavours – nor does it have to be about the loudest voices.

And this is when I imagine my grandmother meeting Anthony Bourdain.

It's not a situation most people would game out, but it's something that I've wondered about.

They're not the most obvious companions or hypothetical dinner guests – and their lifetimes had no clear overlap. You'd have to reprogram entire universes to make it happen.

Anthony Bourdain was a culinary thrill-seeker – his border-crossing curiosity took him far beyond the world's glossy tourist spots: the TV presenter and chef underwent security training before entering Kurdistan and famously landed in Beirut to film his *No Reservations* show, only to watch the airport get blown up from his hotel window days later.

So, what does any of this have to do with my grandmother ever hypothetically socialising with him?

Well, let's rewind to the first time I heard about the author of *Kitchen Confidential*. I quickly learned about the punchline stings of his honesty and how much sidelining meat really threw him off-axis. 'Vegetarians are the enemy of everything good and decent in the human spirit, an affront to all I stand for, the pure enjoyment of food,' he wrote in his influential memoir. 'The body, these waterheads imagine, is a temple that should not be polluted by animal protein. It's healthier, they insist, though every vegetarian waiter I've worked with is brought down by any rumor of a cold.'

He probably wasn't the only chef to dunk on vegetarians at the time, and this kind of target practice was probably considered 'edgy' – but the joke already felt tired to me. And I wonder about his quickfire dismissal of someone like my grandmother, how he wrote her off without even really understanding why she'd be a vegetarian for Buddhist reasons – that there's a power to living your beliefs via your dinner plate, via the flavours you choose to portion out. I've eaten Buddhist temple food that is deliberately quite plain and isn't meant to excite or animate the senses. Sometimes your appetite isn't really ripe for a fat-loaded, funk-choked blue cheese. There are many different ways to savour and appreciate food. It's not always about big, blockbuster flavours.

One of the best meals of my life was at a seventeenth-century temple in Kyoto called Kanga-An, which specialises in fucha ryori – a more lavish, flavour-rich extension of shojin ryori, the Zen cuisine that Buddhist monks serve. One of the menu's simplest dishes was a pickled ume tempura that was set in a Japanese pepper-ginger soup. I still can remember the buzz of the pepper-bright, ginger-shot broth, and the fried fritter with its sour-sweet, lip-puckering magic.

Bourdain once said in a *Playboy* interview, 'You're at Grandma's house, you eat what Grandma serves you.' He also said, 'Being a vegan is a first-world phenomenon, completely self-indulgent.' But what about my grandmother's beliefs? Maybe you'd mellow about this if you could sit down to some pan-fried bitter melon with her. I know it's easy to forget about the connection between what we eat and its prior, full-blooded existence. For my grandmother, that was a principle that influenced every dish at her table. All around the world, vegan dishes are a key part of what people eat – whether they're purposely plant-based or accidentally meat-free, because protein is a major luxury or hard to come by.

Perhaps when Bourdain complained about the joylessness of vegan food, he was imagining some health-food stereotype about unseasoned lentil patties and raw celery sticks, or overpriced green juices and sandwiches with a weedy number of sprouts. In Sydney, though, vegan cuisine is so wide-ranging and welcoming, and truly about a constellation of flavours and stories. Just tonight, my friend and I bonded over recollections of vegan bún riêu we slurped from a Buddhist restaurant in Cabramatta. And yesterday, my boyfriend and I shared a payload of dishes from the Sydney Vegan Market: our plates were filled with Creole jambalaya and Ethiopian atakilt wot, which we sponged up with cornbread and injera. There was also a plant-based Philly 'cheese steak' and a classic

Aussie finger bun, bright with frosted-pink icing and rainbow sprinkles. Had we still been hungry, we could have lined up for vegan baklava, Thai street food or much, much more.

Bourdain still is an influential food media figure, long after his tragic death in 2018. Many people have been inspired by his seemingly democratic, upfront and unvarnished attitude to food. He widened the aperture so audiences thought beyond the traditional regions and restaurants that got coverage and made us consider the unsung labour that made our food – stating that immigrants (particularly undocumented workers) were 'the backbone of the industry'.[1] This is all rightfully noteworthy and admirable. But some of his actions haven't aged particularly well: he once called chef Alice Waters 'Pol Pot in a muumuu' – as if there's one-for-one equivalence between being a genocidal dictator and championing farm-to-table dining.

Bourdain's early dismissal of meat-free dining feels premature and a little closed-minded to me. And I'm grateful that attitudes towards vegetarian and vegan food have evolved greatly – there's no longer that rush to make us target practice for long-dated jokes. So many vegan dishes have rich histories – the mock meats that Buddhist monks made, centuries ago, are precursors to the headline-attracting celeriac shawarma at Copenhagen's Noma in 2018 and the Impossible Burgers of today.

The only universe where my grandmother and Bourdain might ever share a meal is the one that exists in my imagination, and in this world she would tell him to maybe lighten up and enjoy her steamed tofu in ginger syrup. Elsewhere, in the real world, I appreciate that his verdict on vegans wasn't the final say on this – that there are chefs and cooks redefining, every day, what plant-based food can be. I know that I'm just footsteps away from trying Ozone's summer vegetable tempura with matcha salt or El Sabbagh's koshari flavoured with garlic vinegar. And I know in this part of Sydney, vegan food is outmatching the people who originally dismissed it.

Eatplaces: Tables Talk of Yesterdays

Scott Alves Barton

Three months after my birth, and four years after the postpartum death of my sister April, my parents and three-year-old brother Craig moved house. From our George Washington Carver apartment on Norwalk's south side, we drove a short 3 miles to integrate into a community sandwiched between the tonier town lines of Westport and Weston. I grew up as 'that Black family in the pink house' on a suburban Connecticut hillside. I shared a bedroom with Craig, whose walls were papered with pink ballerinas. Pink wall-to-wall carpets anchored the living room, bathroom fixtures and our home's exterior, until my parents could afford to change the décor. The original homeowners, one of a few who would sell to a Black family, paid extra for customisation of our pink travesty in Norwalk's premier school district.

Following my parents' deaths I renovated and sold our house. I Goodwill-ed family remnants, catalogued treasures, and gifted memorabilia to cousins. What remained were our sixties faux-Eero Saarinen Formica 'Tulip' kitchen table and the forties stolid mahogany dining set, my maternal grandparents' wedding gift, bought 'on time'. Why hadn't I disposed of these tables, given the imminent sale? Pitching them in the dumpster brought teary cheeks . . . why cry over relics? They were *lieux de mémoire*, familial monuments, patinaed with memories and bygone meals. I was frightened to lose archives of our hearts and minds. To lose these 'rememories' of home as a safe zone in a sometimes-unfriendly world for an integrating Black family – and a child; tween; teen – trying to understand how to cook, how to survive and to just . . . be.

These tables spoke to me of NAACP (National Association for the Advancement of Colored People) meetings, pizza-fuelled candlelit blackouts and marriage proposals. Sitting down to eat measured healthy meals, reflecting Mom's first career in dietetics. She made the kitchen our play centre while she cooked. It had shiny varnished knotty pine cabinets with copper hinges evoking another era. The linoleum floor irked Mom. Its textured gunmetal and off-white tiles always seemed dirty to her. The stove was electric. The two fluorescent ceiling coil fixtures had a pull string. The sink was enamelled porcelain with black trim, and we hadn't yet gotten a dishwasher. In the early seventies everything got renovated.

We began cooking in nursery school, by learning how to make our favourite dishes. One of the first meals I learned how to make was marinara sauce from scratch. And how to portion dry pasta and test when spaghetti was al dente. Sometimes we made meatballs too – ground pork, veal and beef, onions, garlic, egg, breadcrumbs and Italian seasoning. I hated cheese as a kid, so nothing grated on top. Steamed broccoli as a side vegetable, and a simple green salad. Dad regularly made his mother's sweet-sour creamy salad dressing. Then came memories of Mom's menopausal hot flashes extinguishing our dinner. I cried, too young to know what I struggled to understand. The pomp and stress linked to formal holiday meals. Progressive paella dinners and stir-fries in new-ish woks. On-the-go teen meals. The yuk-and-yum of new foods. Taking turns saying grace. Arguments and 'The Talk'.

I will never forget one August luncheon that brought my first crush to the table. Her name was Bonneyclaire and her lace wristlet gloves, sling-back pumps and stockings, seersucker skirt-suit, straw boater and Birmingham drawl made my heart throb. She became my early babysitter and heartthrob. When she received a Quaker fellowship for high school, she lived with our family friends, the Thompsons. Bonneyclaire was gifted surrogate Black godmothers, including Mom. She could have been a fifth 'little girl' that September of 1963 in the 16th Street Baptist Church bombing. She taught me about compassion and Southern life.

Mahogany didn't shy from politics. Whether Dad's Redevelopment Agency board meetings to improve housing and infrastructure, Mom's femicentric organisational strategy meetings for the first local HeadStart program, or the First Women's Bank. It held heated debates between militant educators, union organisers and theorists. Everyone from celebrated activists Doxey and Yolanda Wilkerson to UConn trustees and state representatives sat at that table. We met taxing district chairman, Otha Brown Jr.; chairman of

Westport's Board of Education, Joan Schine; and Fair Housing Commissioner, Heather Rodin, who brought Paul Robeson Jr. in tow. Mom's brother Paget Jr., associate director of the National Urban League, joined us too, as well as leftist-crusaders Uncle Bert and Aunt Carmen, who helped Paul Robeson Sr. survive the blacklist. Mom and I anchored these debates with hot and cold canapés, Dad's sangria, fried chicken, her famous three-cheese baked macaroni or homemade pies. These tables were sites of celebrations and tragedies, 'adult talk' about sex and childbirth, silent treatments, birthdays and repasts. Record-keeping containers of our collective imagination. If only we could hear the thoughts of our household objects, always presumed to be inanimate, ignored, not listened to, and then replaced.

Two Waning Tall Trees

Sylvia, my Mom, transitioned on the winter solstice. Her parting gift: the shortest day, truncated mourning; poesis. In retrospect her passing was a blessing. During her final year I partially moved in: to help out, cook, and give Dad emotional support.

Mom barely ate fish. Dad's coastal Massachusetts roots made seafood his first love. He lacked a dining partner. I got hooked. I'll eat anything that swims. I cooked his favourite seafood dishes, or brought takeaway from treasured restaurants. His tacit lie, 'Not hungry. I ate while you were out . . .' I persuaded him to eat a few gambas al ajillo on his ninetieth birthday. While he was eating, his neurologist pulled me aside to recommend hospice.

Surprisingly, in home hospice Dad wanted an ultradry

Martini. A filmy kiss of Noilly Prat Vermouth. Syrupy Tanqueray pulled from the freezer. Ice unnecessary: just olives. Dad, thin and weak, propped up on too many pillows, sniffed, swirled and sucked his glass dry. He slept for forty-eight hours. Open secret: his end was beginning.

He had a stroke thirteen days ago, driving to get me at MetroNorth. Ten days before his birthday. He passed eight weeks later; on Mom's birthday. He refused to eat until lack took him. Cliff became Sylvia's ultimate romantic birthday gift; if hereafter exists.

Once they had both passed, everyone advised home renovation. 'It'll improve the market value' became my rear-view grieving project: a visceral reflection of our homelife. Kitchen demolition revealed forgotten layers of tile, linoleum, wallpapers, Dad's fixit projects; more memories. Joys to near failures: lopsided cakes, crunchy icing, handmade holiday decorations, frenzied teenage bread baking, archaic TV series: *Astro Boy, Krazy Kat, Howdy Doody, Sea Hunt*; tremulous as lightning. The rotary wall phone's extra-long cord facilitating tableside conversations. Food and cooking were our touchstones, the glue revealing the tables' resonance.

Our home now nearly empty . . . ready for staging: neutralised. It went from a beating heart to an inanimate object. If only walls could talk – or how about if tables could do the same? If the mahogany or Tulip tables spoke, what stories would they share?

Tulip Times

The 'pre-Tulip' kitchen table was a reminder of our old life in Norwalk. An oval beige-and-chrome Formica, junked between LBJ's 1964 War on Poverty, King's Selma-to-Montgomery March, and the 1965 north-eastern blackout, when Dad improvised a makeshift fridge from a camping cooler.

Dad went from English teacher to speech pathologist to Westport's assistant school superintendent. Suddenly, dinners happened in restaurants. Frequently we were conveniently forgotten 'dining while Black' when meetings delayed Dad. Passive-aggressive maître d's trying to convince Mom to leave, which only made her more intransigent. Dad had a public face. Tokenised? Perhaps. When he arrived, a table had 'been ready all along' – so they said. Those fractured meals hung in our throats. Dad's promotion meant the removal of everything pink, heralding the Tulip's arrival with its white wrought iron chairs and turquoise vinyl cushioned seats.

Dad brought it home after work, which meant that John's Best pizza was its inaugural meal. Tulip was command central as Albert Shanker led the 1968 NYC-UFT in the Ocean Hill-Brownsville teachers' strike. Blacks, Jews, educators, union and NAACP members, and multiracial friends came to eat, argue and strategise throughout the walkout. After-school snacks became supercharged.

Our daily routine revolved around the Tulip. I was thin and anaemic – the remedy came after breakfasts when Dad and I shared shots of prune juice, or cod liver oil. Both were NASTY. In a drawer near the table was an old leather belt, and a hairbrush. Mom brushed my hair after the breakfast shots against my wishes. On bad days our hands grasped her chairback as she strapped our shins. Decades later she denied those punishments.

After school, Mom and I spent my post-elementary school

afternoons at the Tulip, reading books after snacks. Every summer a cadre of Black labourers stripped and re-tarred our street. I ran outside to touch the cooling hot tar. We offered them our bathroom, made fresh lemonade and sandwiches. Mom wanted them to escape the summer sun, and feel welcome.

And at dinner I slid unwanted food onto the napkin on my lap, then into the trash (they knew). Sunday mornings Dad brought coffeecake or turnovers. After grace, they sat on the Tulip, off limits until vegetables were eaten. Annually, Mom's mom, Grandma 'Jean', Eugenia Constance Alves, came to visit. We cooked Bajan *homefood* together.

One of these were Johnny Cakes, a sweetened fried dough the size of a biscuit. Cousin to Southern Hoe Cakes, and unlike the white cornmeal versions Dad grew up on. Later for dinner standing on a stool I'd help Grandma Jean make chicken-n-rice casserole, escovitch fish, or 'fungie aka coucou', a moulded okra and cornmeal pudding. If I was lucky, she'd make us cocobread too.

The fifth seat round the table was needed in the mid-sixties when Vincent Okechuku Ikeh, our 'adopted' Nigerian brother, arrived. UNESCO brought dozens of Ghanaian and Nigerian men to study in US colleges. My godparents and other activist Black families were targeted to serve as surrogate families. Vincent told Igbo stories, and gave me my first dashiki and kufi over dinner.

All the while, kitchen chores rotated weekly. One brother helped cook. The other cleaned. I did what I could until Mom came home to help finish. One summer, I collated her favourite recipes. We spread cookbooks and filecards over the Tulip for meal planning and recipe analysis.

One evening while we were sat around the Tulip, the front doorbell rang. But as no one answered the front door unless we had a party or meeting, or someone like a vacuum cleaner salesman or Tupperware lady came calling, he eventually walked to our kitchen door, which was used as the main entrance and closest to the driveway. A tall white man, business suit and overcoat. A stranger to everyone, I thought; not to Craig. Apologising for the interruption, he walked in. 'Mr Barton, I think we have a problem.' Mom's eyes shot overtop her eyeglasses, sinking just as rapidly. 'I am Kim's father.' He motioned to the French doors behind Dad. 'Perhaps we could sit down in your living room and talk, man to man.' Kim's family were fellow St Paul's Episcopal congregants. We'd integrated there to honour Mom's Church of England roots. Kim's family lived in a WASP-y enclave of old stone-hewn homes across town.

As a speech pathologist Dad had impeccable linguistics, which had suddenly morphed into a slippery elliptical rhetoric of dropped consonants and lazy vowels. 'We haasa problem? I dunt see one . . .' Uncharacteristically blackened English. 'I think you know why I am here. It's about my daughter. And your son.' Two fathers talked at each other. Craig squirmed. Dinner became icy. This was the first of several interracial encounters for my brother.

Long before we thought about dating, Mom had given her version of 'The Talk' following *Ebony*'s publications: 'The Home life of Mai Britt and "Golden Boy"' (December 1964) and 'Is My Mixed Marriage Mixing Up My Kids?' (October 1966). Although we had an integrated community and multiracial friends, dating and eventual marriage would face insurmountable challenges if we did what Sammy Davis Jr. did.

Our dad wouldn't capitulate to Kim's dad's harangues. The side-door slammed. Dress shoes crunched on gravel. He sped away in his Lincoln. Craig cried, ran to his room. Mom followed. Romance over.

Mr Mahogany

High school homework pushed me onto the larger dining room table. Mom disapproved. I promised to work overtop the leather and velveteen table pad, not on the mirror finish tabletop. Her Greek Revival table was a wedding gift and sat on fluted cabriolet 'antiqued' ivory legs, complemented by six upholstered vermilion and gold brocade chairs. Middle-class aspirational. One day, I marred Mahogany, ruining its finish. Later hot irons scarred party linens and Mahogany. Mom scolded me, 'Sc-ot-tie! Scott. Alves. Barton. Pay attention – look at what you've done!'

Summer white sales meant hunting for damask table-cloths, candlesticks, linen napkins to complement Mom's trophy. Tabletop décor included sprays of candy-apple bittersweet stark against winter's snows, homemade tchotchkes, antique-y bric-a-brac and candle's glow. Whenever Mom's decorating designs needed support, Dad would build or jury-rig it. Their teamwork paid off. Before I left for college, we found china and glassware satisfying Mom's decorator dreams. I salvaged the dining room's only vestige, Dad's thrifted antique chandelier.

I cooked prom dinners and after-prom breakfasts for teen friends. The dinners were designed to be easy to eat and not saucy to damage our fancy outfits. Roast chicken and rosemary potatoes, asparagus from Dad's garden, soft drinks, homemade dinner rolls and cake, not pie. For the breakfasts, a steaming stainless percolator sat tableside although most of us hadn't yet embraced coffee. Dad either made waffles or his buttermilk pancakes with fresh maple syrup. Mom would make coffeecake or a stollen with fresh fruit. Scrambled or fried eggs were made to order. The final touches were a platter of crispy bacon and sausage links, and a pitcher of freshly squeezed OJ. Intoxication or overly amorous liaisons anchored those sobering cook-ups. Mahogany hosted Craig's engagement party, cousins Buff and Susan's wedding rehearsal dinners. Mom's annual family BBQ, job promotions and retirement parties swung between the porch and Mahogany. Sly, Duke and Nina provided vibes.

Following my French apprenticeships, I created a fête with foie gras, black truffles, rabbit roulade, chocolate desserts and complementary wine pairings. Mom's eighty-seventh birthday party was her final shindig. In attendance were both of her sisters, Hazel (now 102) and Ruth, her 'spiritsista' – or sister-in-law – Carmen, and my cousins. We ate, laughed, drank and *talkedstory* around Mahogany. Mom waved her minions farewell on her electrified stair-chair in a ceremonial cape, bejewelled plastic crown, sceptre in hand. Our tables were repositories of our social and commensal history.

Post-mortem

Mahogany has groaned with funerary repasts. Following Sylvia's public memorial. Then, at her one-year anniversary, my childhood BFF Jill, my partner Michele and cousins Chris and Lisa cheered our whisper-quiet home. Tulip marked vigils with pizza boxes during Dad's hospice. Mahogany went mute. Its last meal was a simple repast following his memorial service. Brief reminiscences. Flat affect; joylessness garnished with Chinese takeout.

The house went to contract. It was emptied of materiality and memories. Neither table would fit in my apartment. Craig already had a furnished life in Virginia. I couldn't imagine discarding these stalwart soldiers at Goodwill. Metonymies of our family's integration in 'that' pink house. Archiving foodways. And our family's culture. All our yesterdays. Simulacra proxies for angel parents. Precious memories embedded in wood and Formica.

A Black congregation in Bridgeport welcomed recent immigrant families with new-to-gently-used furniture. I never met the Mexican family that received Mahogany. The faux-Saarinen went to a friend of a friend's adult child. I don't know how long a life either of our former 'family members' had. Hopefully they live as grace notes. Commensal hearts in someone else's homes.

Why Black Spaces Are Needed in an Industry That Refuses to Change

Selasie Dotse

18 October 2016. The first Soul Food Sessions dinner had just concluded and I had never felt more alive as a young cook. I looked around and saw nothing but Black faces in the kitchen and I realised what I had been missing my entire career . . . true acceptance, representation and inclusion. The hip-hop bumped in the dining room. The chefs cooked with a swag I didn't think was allowed in a kitchen. There was no pressure to one-up one another. It was just good vibes. It was fun and exciting. It reminded me of why I loved cooking. I felt like I had found my tribe, my people, my family.

Unlike in the other kitchens we had worked in, our Blackness was celebrated. I've been trying to chase the high from that night ever since. I've worked in countless restaurants and for several 'woke' chefs, but never have I felt that same sense of belonging. Hospitality is a white supremacist industry run by white cis men. The only solution for Black folks to 'get a seat at the table' is for us to create our own table. We need to focus less on trying to fit into these white spaces that were never designed for us and focus more on creating our own spaces that will uplift us.

Verbally abusing and berating staff. Exploitation. Paying staff poverty wages. Little to no paid sick time or healthcare benefits. These are the unethical, white supremacist work practices that most restaurants are steeped in. Having to navigate this toxic culture in addition to the anti-Blackness I experience daily at restaurants has taken a toll on me physically, emotionally, mentally and spiritually. There are days when I feel so overwhelmed by hopelessness in this work that it is difficult for me to get out of bed. Anxiety attacks before work are a regular occurrence. Intrusive negative thoughts and self-doubt about my skills, abilities and efforts as a chef are debilitating. The heaviness of being a Black chef in this industry is monumental. There are a number of things that weigh most heavily on me.

Isolation

I've spent sixteen years in the hospitality industry. I've worked in many restaurants, from quick service to Michelin, in the South and in the San Francisco Bay Area. I've dedicated my entire career to the industry, but never felt like I mattered or belonged. I've often been the only Black chef or cook in an establishment. The more high-end the establishment, the fewer Black faces there are. Being the only Black chef in a restaurant means experiencing a significant amount of microaggressions. Using AAVE in a mocking or joking manner doesn't make you cool. Playing hip-hop, rap or R&B in spaces where you don't have any Black employees makes me side-eye you. Expressing that 'you're not a racist, but . . .' definitely makes you a racist. Non-Black chefs of colour aren't any better and also perpetuate anti-Black microaggressions. I'd like to believe that all chefs of colour are in the same struggle against racism and white supremacy, but anti-Blackness is universal and many of these POC 'allies' aren't taking the time to look at their own biases against Black folks. Being the only Black chef in many restaurants, nobody really has my back because nobody really understands what I'm experiencing. I don't have the needed support to back me when something is said or done that makes me uncomfortable. It's exhausting.

Tokenisation and Fetishisation

Hospitality activist and advocate Ashtin Berry says, 'Tokenization functions as a form of performative solidarity. It asks the question: "How can we LOOK inclusive?" rather than "How do we BECOME inclusive?"'[1] When I'm one of the only (or, in fact, the only) Black employees in a restaurant, it's hard not to feel like I'm filling someone's quota. But diversity hires are BS as they do not equate to inclusion. As someone who's Black, queer, gender non-conforming and an African immigrant, I check a lot of diversity boxes. But I am not a spokesperson for all those groups. Black people, like any other ethnic or cultural group, are not a monolith. The intersection of my race, gender and gender expression has made me vulnerable to sexual harassment and fetishising. Because of my gender expression, a chef once asked me what restroom I use. I felt empowered to do little more than roll my eyes and continue working. Another chef repeatedly asked to touch my hair despite me telling him no every time. Many cooks have made attempts to flirt with me and ask me inappropriate questions about my sexuality. I've had cooks ask to have sex with me to 'try out' men or have had hugs that linger too long. Most of the time, I awkwardly laugh it off or roll my eyes. When I attempt to confront these behaviours I am told that I am 'uptight'.

Codeswitching

Having to codeswitch in order to make other people feel comfortable is exhausting. What I've learned is that showing my genuine emotions is unacceptable. When I express joy or excitement I'm seen as 'loud and boisterous'. When I'm firm and assertive I'm told that I'm 'mean' or 'intimidating'. Displaying confidence and self-assurance is seen as 'cocky' (code for 'uppity'). Expressing frustration or annoyance, even in the face of racism, is seen as 'having an attitude'. Using AAVE as a non-Black person is received as funny or hip. But when I, an actual Black person, use AAVE I'm seen as 'unintelligent' or 'ghetto'. Having to codeswitch to make myself a palatable Black person forces me to hide my authentic self. This hiding stifles my creativity and self-expression as a chef.

Perfectionism

The hospitality industry, in particular fine dining restaurants, stresses the importance of perfection. When I worked at Lazy Bear, everything from the base ingredients, to our prepped components, to the plating and even garnishes had to be as perfect as possible. The constant societal pressure instilled in me from my parents and former Black authoritative figures in my life of having to 'be better' and 'perform better' than my white counterparts in order to receive any kind of recognition or career mobility has been distressing. And this pressure is compounded even further by feeling like the representative of an entire race of people.

I remember when I worked at SPQR in San Francisco, the executive chef was talking with myself and the kitchen staff and during the conversation stated that 'Africans don't have drinkable tap water in their homes.' I was shocked to hear such a 'progressive' white man say something like that. As the resident Black and African employee, I felt I had no choice but to speak up and call out the falseness in his statement. This led to a back-and-forth argument between myself and the chef, where despite my best efforts, I wasn't able to convince him that Africans in fact do have drinkable tap water.

Another memory: at Lazy Bear, while I was in the prep kitchen picking herbs for dinner service, I said to the other chef de partie I was working with, 'If you don't look at the clock, time goes by faster.' 'You should say that in an African accent,' said the executive chef who was standing nearby. I stopped picking the herbs and looked at him, unable to believe what I had just heard. 'What'd you say?' I asked. 'That phrase is perfect for an African accent: "In my country, time goes by faster if you don't look at the clock,"' he said in a fake African accent. I was stunned. I laughed awkwardly, shook my head and returned to picking herbs. Later, my non-Black colleagues who witnessed this exchange asked why I hadn't challenged the guy. But I think to myself: why hadn't they? As the only Black and African chef, and after my experience with the executive chef at SPQR, I didn't feel safe or comfortable enough to speak up in these moments because

I didn't want to be portrayed as the 'unruly' or 'disruptive' Black employee.

Because I didn't feel comfortable or like any of my colleagues had my back, I felt like I couldn't make any mistakes. A mistake could mean my downfall, and that's exactly what happened. I was fired from Lazy Bear for forgetting to prep a sauce and for dropping my gougères before service. The official notice said I was terminated for not being prepared for service, but I saw it as being terminated for making a couple of mistakes. This desire and need for perfection has only exacerbated my anxiety as a chef. Perfection is the standard and perfection means grace for mistakes is rarely – if ever – doled out.

The spaces where I've felt the most supported, accepted and celebrated during my culinary career were Black spaces. Participating in events like Soul Food Sessions, the BayHaven Food and Wine Festival and the Black Food & Wine Experience, as well as collaborating with Bay Area Black business owners and chefs such as Bryant Terry, Molly Bradshaw, Geoff Davis, Nelson German and Edwin Bayone III, has given me an inner peace and sense of belonging in the industry that I never thought was possible.

The Soul Food Sessions dinner series was a series of dinners in Charlotte, North Carolina started by a group of local Black chefs and business owners that served to highlight and promote Black chefs and mixologists in the Charlotte metro area due to the lack of representation of Black chefs in the media. It played a momentous role in helping me find my voice and confidence as a chef. I met Chef Gregory Collier, a founding chef of Soul Food Sessions, when I was interviewing for a breakfast cook position at his cafe. After sharing my frustrations about being a Black chef in the industry, Greg invited me to hang out with him and the other chefs during the inaugural Soul Food Sessions dinner. At that dinner, I met the rest of the crew: Chef Michael Bowling, Chef Gregory Williams, Chef Jamie Barnes and Pastry Chef Jamie Turner. This incredible group of chefs quickly became my mentors. For the second Soul Food Sessions dinner, the chefs invited me back to the team and asked me to present my own dish for a course. I was encouraged to present a dish that represented me. My entire career, I had felt unsure and insecure about cooking the African food I had grown up with. But with the encouragement of my mentors, I decided, 'Fuck it. Why not? I'm with family.' I presented a variation of Ghanaian waakye which received glowing reviews. I continued to participate in the Soul Food Sessions dinner series until I moved to the San Francisco Bay Area in 2018. Being an active member of this Black chef collective gave me the confidence boost I needed to finally leave North Carolina and move to California.

Since moving to the San Francisco Bay Area, I've found solace and joy in doing pop-up dinners and events with Serigne Mbaye, Nelson German, Bryant Terry, Geoff Davis, Molly Bradshaw's team at Mission Bowling Club, and the team at Café Colucci. Working with other Black chefs has continuously reminded me that Black spaces are the only spaces where I feel affirmed and supported. It is also important for me to build and curate my own spaces for Black chefs and Black food. In August 2020, I launched e le aḍe [Elade] Test Kitchen (fka Sankofa), a Ghanaian dinner series. In October 2020, I organised and facilitated a virtual discussion panel, 'Black in Hospitality', in collaboration with African American Student Development at the University of California, Berkeley. Currently, I'm in the process of creating a dinner series focused on highlighting Black hospitality professionals: chefs, sommeliers, mixologists, etc.

Through my experiences in the hospitality industry, I have learned that as Black folks, we cannot rely on white industry leaders, employers and employees to unlearn white supremacy, white privilege and create safe spaces for Black employees. White people are too comfortable with their privilege and are unwilling to give it up. White supremacy is strongly ingrained in this country and this industry. We cannot wait for organisations to make Black employees feel like they belong. We cannot wait for anti-racism and DEI training initiatives to be implemented in organisational mandates and strategic plans. We cannot wait for intentional hiring practices to roll out and for complaints and concerns about racism in the workplace to be prioritised and addressed.

As Black folks, we have always created spaces for ourselves, our families and our communities. These spaces have been a vital resource during social movements and are necessary for our safety and survival. These spaces build community and belonging so we can be our true selves and have a support system. Encouragement and guidance through mentorship becomes a reality in these spaces. Access to upward mobility for leadership and management positions becomes possible in these spaces.

Black people: we can and have been supporting and uplifting ourselves for millennia, and we'll continue to do so as long as it's necessary. Spending our energy being angry or fighting against people who have no interest in seeing us succeed is a waste of energy. And energy is a finite resource. The best use of that energy is to put it into people that will support us, and that can only be us. Black liberation and joy in hospitality starts and ends with us. We must take care of us.

Find Your People

Mavis-Jay Sanders

I've been in proximity to coverups all my life. I'm not on the Olivia Pope level, but masking the truth for a better story that ensures your survival is first nature to any adolescent queer-identifying person of colour born indoctrinated into and by a conservative religion. Through experience and careful observation, I learned my place: where to stand out, where to hide, and how to steer clear of the ceiling. No one knows the rules better than someone trying to survive. I had to discover barriers to carve out the safe spaces that would allow me to be honest about how I felt and what I was experiencing. Creating those spaces for myself inevitably attracted others in search of solace, community and nourishment. When you don't belong to one specific mainstream identity, you get to live life from the perspective of many. I think of it as intersectional privilege. Over time I've accumulated niche communities of people who hold multiple identities at once. Because of this, I've been known to have all the tea.

One of my favourite forms of connectivity in life is a group chat. There's continuous and immediate connection. You can reach out with a random idea or experience and have people weigh in to assist, validate or correct a train of thought, share a joke or have instant support for an awkward moment. It's like having a lifeline in your back pocket at all times. The pool of people can be as defined as you want it to be, and you can have as many groups in your community as you need. There's the general family group chat (mutually exclusive from the generational cousins group chats); chefs of colour who're from a specific restaurant; restaurant general managers in New York City; food policy folks; Black queer hospitality femmes; peers from an alma mater; powerful older white women mentors; my besties; the dinner gang.

I am part of one group thread in particular which really feeds me. It's made up of a special combination of colleagues who've all either formerly worked or currently work at some iteration of the same restaurant group. One afternoon as I sat in my car, my phone buzzed with a call from a member of the executive team at one of these restaurants (a former place of employment of mine). As it was someone I'd admired and had fond memories of, I didn't hesitate to accept the call. After pleasantries and a brief catch-up, they unveiled the real reason for the call: interviews were being conducted around an alleged scandal that had taken place at the establishment. They had questions:

Did you know about the article?
Yes.

Has someone from the press contacted you?
Yes.
Have you spoken to, or do you intend on speaking with, a reporter?
No.
Will you go on record refuting any allegations that come against the establishment?

. . .

Naturally, when I got off the call I jumped onto the group chat of former employees. Everyone had been called; not everyone was inclined to pick up the phone. Those who had were asked the same questions. Following this interaction, I began to understand two things more clearly:

1. I have the ability to influence people in my professional community and I have power that I can wield in various situations.

2. I would have to be more discerning about who I allow to influence me.

While I hold no ill will towards anyone involved in this situation, I have made the decision to minimise my communications with anyone who chose to answer that last question, 'Yes.'

People who benefit from toxic restaurant practices have said employees knew what they were getting themselves into, going to work there. Working in restaurants in general can be dangerous: they are ultimately white male-dominated spaces, not known for supporting or nurturing much of anything other than egos and addictions. The truth is, we knew there were dangers, but there's no way of knowing the extent of danger and what you could lose until you've experienced it. The power of the people telling you it's OK outweighs the few voices raising red flags. There's an arrogance that comes with youth.

Growing up in the South with an uncle who played professional baseball, I was privy to first-hand stories of what it was like to play a national sport during the time of integration. Over and over again, I heard older men go on and on about how the player who broke the colour line wasn't the greatest Black baseball player, he was just positioned best to be accepted by white dominant culture: he had the best temperament, resilience, discipline, willingness to assimilate and play to respectability politics.

These days I often wonder, is the Black community delusional if they continue to put stock in the concept of incremental progress? At one time, it was likely the most effective non-physically violent way for large-scale progress to change the image of Blacks as a whole. As much as I hate to admit it, Black America is still in a time where we are counting firsts. As Black people, we've created, defined and been on the cutting edge of culture in every avenue. Against all odds we continue to contribute, create and redefine. The scarcity mindset of 'there will only be *one*: the first' has to die.

Ultimately we'll find ourselves at a collective loss when we excuse, defend and cover up just to keep that *one*. As we do in restaurant culture, we give ourselves over in these situations to the promise of power and of proximity to it. When it all goes wrong the predatory people shift the blame over and put accountability on the person who has the least amount of power in the scenario.

Granted, there are more opportunities for the success and visibility of different types of Black people, though credit has to be marginal in comparison to contribution. But at what cost? Who pays the price? And if they knew the true exchange, would they agree that the price was worth it? If not, are you not perpetuating the same harm you say that you're fighting?

As with so many restaurant colleagues, I know how subjective any scenario can be. I've experienced a scenario where one person will say, 'No, this is exploitative,' and another will say, 'Thank God this is so much better than my last situation.' And this is not only applicable to this profession; this is the lens through which anyone in a non-dominant identity sees every situation they're in. For all the work I and so many others have put into creating self-spaces for ourselves and our communities, they are liminal. We exist and operate in spaces that aren't created for or by us.

Sometimes, even those we feel we should be in alignment with abuse their power. At a large-scale food festival, I was enjoying an after-hours gathering with the other chefs when a gentleman approached me and the young woman I was speaking with. A fellow Black chef, a person of note and high regard; it seemed as though he and I should have an inborn camaraderie, an understanding. Instead, he launched into an unsolicited monologue about how he didn't understand why it might bother my companion if he just came out and told her he thought she was attractive.

Another Black female chef stepped in to educate this gentleman. Shortly after, he apologised. He is of an older generation. To others, it may seem like too much to learn, or unfair. Unfair to be called out. Unfair for times to have changed the rules. Unfair to be expected to adapt. But if you hold yourself as a person of value committed to the progression of people, then you should understand that you may have a blind spot that is standing in the way of you leaving the legacy you strive for. It's OK to give the helm over to younger people. To invite the new generation with opposing views in. They may teach you a thing or two that can help you navigate the social change that is on the horizon. Let go of your power before it takes you out. Unlike the scenario above, this proves difficult for many; in kitchen culture, it's nearly unheard of.

But there's more nuance there. It's the culturing of generations of chefs in the toxic brigade system. It's the glee consumers find in the explosions of famous white male chefs, the meek 'yes, chef' that meets the profanity-laced rant about a dish served in an imaginary dining room, for faux guests, all for a camera. It's the pervasiveness of entitled thinking that corrupts leaders, who believe their power is absolute and can only be sullied by distributing it to others. People aren't good and bad. There are no absolutes one way or another, but we can make better decisions. As new thought leaders come into power, it's important not to get stuck on 'that's just how it is'. We should be approaching our systems, tasks, relationships, everything in a way that redefines what's possible for all those affected by what we're building both as workers and those in need of the services provided. It's how all the catalysing characters of a progressive movement have made a lasting impact.

Someone's ability to curate a futuristic dining experience or to have an impact on policy and agriculture does not nullify facilitating poor culture between staff and employees. When their grand vision compromises the wellness and drive of their colleagues, that too is part of their lasting impact: the 'power over' rather than 'power with' mindset is what their legacy will eventually be distilled into. But we're human, and imperfect, and we admire who we admire, for whatever reasons. Who a leader is to one person does not hold weight for every person, but that belief is still valid.

We have to allow space for both truths to exist in order to be able to rectify this scenario.

We have to let go of the good–bad binary in order for progress to ensue.

We have to be leaders who are flawed, but who are perpetually working towards better, asking more of ourselves, our colleagues and our industries.

Intersectional privilege has given me a greater opportunity to see this than most. My intersectional identity, however, has suffered at the inability of many to grasp it. This is why I lead as I do; this is why I challenge others to be aware of their own identities and privileges. I had to learn the rules to survive. I wish that everyone would task themselves with learning them, so that we all may thrive instead.

Society has to stop demanding perfection of an authority. It's a set-up for failure. It's unrealistic to expect people to be all things to all people at once, which means that by our nature of existence we are continuously in opposition to what someone else believes is correct. Opposing opinions should be able to exist without destroying others. What's harmful is when you remove a person's free will and try to impose a way of life on them. What we must demand instead is accountability: both of our leaders, and for those under their guidance.

There is an enormous pressure felt by younger generations to play into the precedent set by problematic leaders. If a person of power invites you to their table and there's a rumoured scandal surrounding them, can you engage and learn from them without contributing to the problem? It should be possible, and yet tremendous barriers are being constructed around the opportunity. Fear of retaliation and being discredited for being honest are genuine concerns. What if that means we're losing the real change agents with integrity because they know they cannot safely engage with these problematic leaders and escape with their own reputations unscathed? People should not be collateral damage for the success of others. Learn from your elders, sure, but take note of their faults and foibles and scandals, as well as the knowledge they impart. Those who currently hold the most power are deeply flawed. As dynamics shift and the old guard loses its stranglehold on influence, the identities of the power holders will change, but the human nature of being imperfect will not. So, we task ourselves now to be mindful of this truth, and build ourselves and our communities to be better, stronger, more aware, more accountable, and ultimately more capable of using our power for progress.

It can be easy to lose hope, as the faces of those who continue to determine the course of our lives seem to remain unwaveringly the same. But your collaborators and co-conspirators are out there in a group chat, as hungry and devoted as you are. The pockets of people who will hold space for you exist and are worth waiting for. Don't let lost hope and a compromise stop you from meeting the groups of people you were actually hoping to collaborate and build with in the first place. Continue to do your work with all the integrity, brilliance and care that you can bring. And soon enough, with diligence and patience, you'll have a new group chat: eager to grow, tackle challenges together, and perpetually thirsting for your best tea.

Your Hands Look Different Now

Chris Nigro

You watch your hands change under a meat slicer. They have more veins and they are larger now. You start to recognise your reflection in the deli bathroom. You hold your hands under the slicer and catch the cheese that falls. They feel the same, but your hands move faster. You flip eggs faster. You soak up the heat under the grill with ease now. You keep catching cheese and ham sliced as thin as possible for the customers at the deli. Arguably the biggest difference is treatment from the other side of the grill by deli folk, customers and staff alike. You are inexperienced. You are still inexperienced. Yet you are treated like you understand more. You are doing the same thing. You are slicing meat and flipping eggs for the classic NYC deli bacon, egg and cheese sandwich. You start to feel more comfortable. You can let your guard down now at night when a crowd comes in after a night of partying. You don't need to defend your skill as much. Drunk men nod at you with respect after you hand them a greasy bacon, egg and cheese and ring them up for a slushie. You don't need to fear a lingering customer wandering the store. You have the same instinct. You feel the same gut-wrenching fear as you bleach down the slicer, wipe the counters and shut the register late at night. You are alone still, but you are safer. Your masculinity is shielding you. They don't know anymore. You are seven months on testosterone. You watch your hands change. You can let your guard down and you keep flipping eggs.

In understanding gender, you grow fixated on constant distraction. You find solace in the repetitive motions that by nature follow cooking. Only as your hands assemble the food you are preparing are you able to unpack the intricacies of the effect gender has had on your life.

You think back to working with food full time for the first time. You ran the coffee counter inside a larger restaurant and you shucked oysters at the same restaurant across the way with your best friend. You picked up jobs together and got a lot more responsibility than you were necessarily qualified for, but amid a pandemic and ongoing food labour shortages they threw you in. You ran with it. You took the money slipped in your back pocket as your insides churn. You and your best friend kept laughing. You weaponised your femininity together. Did you despise it? Sort of, but using it gave you a leg up. You winked at male customers. You made them feel special. You'd let them talk. You'd let them start their mornings with the pretty girls at the coffee bar. They were still talking, you'd let them. You played the role so well you lost track of yourself. They are probably still talking.

You're at another breakfast joint now. You shorten your name. You live in between the binaries of the gender roles that gave you those same perks a few months prior. Things are different. You move cautiously and slowly. You don't want their discomfort to affect you. You sense their fear. You feel their confusion, or hatred, or discontent with your presentation. You accidentally let the past in when you smile a little too comfortably at a male customer. It's a hot cup of coffee thrown back at you. They don't want your attention now. They do not want to be associated with whatever you are. You are not sure what you are. You have not been exposed to people like you before. You never struggled before in undressing yourself. In changing your presentation it's not the immediate relief you expect, but a continual unlearning of the inescapable binaries you are between. You hear more hateful things escape the mouths of the men you work for. You keep creating new food. You assemble more complicated menus. You get to work with fresh produce you haven't been exposed to and learn to smoke meat for grit bowls. You focus on the food. Amid the chaos of a rush you feel sane. You are living to understand now. You are unpacking a lifetime of misunderstanding. More importantly you can bite back now. You can earn respect from those you work for with consistency and time. You thrive on the consistency of schedule. You watch a bullet list of goals for the day get checked off, prepped and sent out to customers. You watch a kitchen that looks destroyed become pristine and brand new within the same nine hours. You get asked weird and inherently personal questions on your body. You don't know what you are aspiring to do. You are questioned. You ask yourself why you want so badly to be what you have despised for so long. Your relationships change. You feel limited in expressing the same joys of your femininity. You struggle in building connections. You are on edge in sharing yourself in fear of becoming predatory.

You hold your hands under the slicer and catch the cheese that falls. You are inexperienced. You are still inexperienced. You will continue to learn. You will bend between the binaries of your gender and use it to create. You will foster new relationships with authenticity. The trans experience has never been bound to cisnormative gender roles, but it has been challenging them for far longer than you have been here. To be trans is to unlearn every gendered experience you come across and act with intention. You will no longer use your transness as a definition, but to bridge the unexplainable in both identity and magic of food. You will move with your food. You will work with your hands to learn. You will foster new relationships you have longed for. Food has been a vessel for transformation and creativity far longer than you. You will look at your hands and recognise them.

Afterword

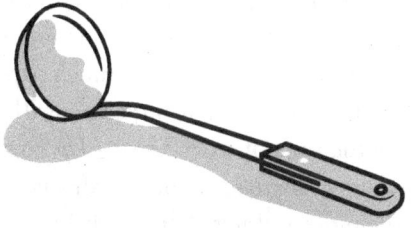

The idea for *Serving Up* was born from a fire for 'fixing'. That fire hasn't quelled within me; it has, however, mutated somewhat. The original intention for this anthology was to bring together a collection of essays on food, identity and culture exploring the intersections between the personal and the political when it comes to food.

Gathering participants for this anthology was simple at first, but it quickly became a case of trying to herd cats. Many of those cats became strays. For one reason or another the original line-up, one by one, made their apologies for not having the time to commit to the project or couldn't meet the deadlines because life was happening.

In the interim I too became overburdened, working a full-time job while also running my business and making appearances at conferences, events and festivals. I dropped the ball. Deliberately. I was not in a place to convene anyone and was going through a long season of depression throughout 2021 and 2022. Hence the delays in this publication.

So this collection, forcibly shifted over the time it has taken to piece together since its inception, is its own perfect storm. Divinely timed in a drought of truth telling, it draws attention to an abandonment of conscious leadership and harrowing levels of mental health crisis permeating workers in hospitality, farming and agriculture and food media. Consumers of food en masse are, too, very much part of the fray.

I am so proud of every voice included here. They each perfectly illustrate the tone of what *Serving Up* now represents: serving up the new vanguard in food media, largely unrepresented and therefore unfiltered by celebrity attachment or award-hunting, simply eager to share and speak their truth without victimhood and inviolable vulnerability.

This collection represents the determined dissonance and disobedience all societies need – these voices tell the truth of their experience and perspective at their own cost to empower and embolden a new consciousness. Themes of psychological safety in the workplace, mental health, grief, sisterhood and queerness dominate the foray into these forensic insights from a diverse collection of voices, while food on film flips the lens on what and where food can influence community and consciousness.

Collectively we say fuck the status quo. Thank you for helping us, through your patronage, in doing so. Thank you for your patience.

Zoe Adjonyoh
May 2024

About the Authors

Zoe Adjonyoh has been cooking up consciousness since 2010. She is an author, entrepreneur and empowerment coach and has spent thirteen years in the hospitality industry focusing on food justice and female empowerment. As the chef and founder of the West African food brand and cookbook Zoe's Ghana Kitchen, Zoe pioneered West African cuisine globally. And through her activism with Black Book Global, Zoe led the conversation on decolonising the food industry. She has previously spoken at TedX and lectured at institutions including Harvard, the Culinary Institute of America, Bates College and the Omega Institute. She was formerly the Director of the Women's Leadership programmes at the James Beard Foundation. Zoe is the author of *Zoe's Ghana Kitchen* and the editor for *Serving Up: Essays on food, identity and culture*. @zoeadjonyoh, @ghanakitchen.

Yasmin Khan is a writer and cook from London who loves to share people's stories through food. An avid traveller whose passport is never too far from her pocket, she runs cooking classes, pop-up supper clubs and writing retreats around the world. Prior to immersing herself in the fragrances and flavours of the Persian kitchen, Yasmin worked as a human rights campaigner, running national and international campaigns for NGOs and grassroots groups, with a special focus on the Middle East. Yasmin's three glorious and thought-provoking cookbooks *The Saffron Tales*, *Zaitoun* and *Ripe Figs* are published by Bloomsbury. Yotam Ottolenghi describes her recipes as 'a mouthwatering showcase of a beautiful country.' www.yasminkhanstories.com

Samah Dada is a multi-hyphenate TV host and on-air contributor, bestselling author, food blogger and media personality whose passion is to share her diverse perspective on food and cuisine merged with inclusivity and wellness. Samah's goal is to create inventive, plant-forward recipes for everyone to enjoy, drawing from her Indian heritage and inspired by the foodscapes of London, California and New York City. You can find Samah on her Instagram @dadaeats and living in Brooklyn, NY – always in search of the next cup of coffee.

Lenore T. Adkins is a freelance food writer based in Washington, DC who has been eating her way through the District for many years. Her work has appeared in *Food & Wine* magazine, the *Washington Post*, on the James Beard Foundation's blog, and within *Fine Dining Lovers*, *Eater* and elsewhere.

Izzie Ramirez is a culture, climate, community and food writer. She's written for *VICE*, *Bitch Media*, *Jezebel* and more. Izzie is currently the managing editor of *Spoon*

University, where she edits college students writing about food for the first time. She graduated from Columbia's mid-career science journalism programme last spring and was a 2020 NYU grad. When she's not editing, she's usually making salsa.

Yoshivel Elise Chirinos is currently based in Queens, New York, and her love for cinema and cheese toasties led her to King's College London where she earned her Master of Arts in Film Studies. She still holds out hope that this degree will one day provide a return on investment. You can find her on Instagram @keen_idea blissfully eating through New York City.

Fatima 'Fatti' Tarkleman is a zero-waste British migrant chef of mixed African-Asian descent. She has special interests in cross-cultural cooking that prioritises sustainability, inclusivity and local produce, while representing her London upbringing, the flavours of her heritage and her travels. She embraces innovative ways of using age-old techniques to provide delicious food, putting care for people, their stories and nature at the heart of her practice. Fatti is currently working on a cookbook that spotlights women and gender queer people of colour and the person who inspired them to cook, working together to create recipes that target household food waste reduction.

Cynthia Greenlee is an intentionally independent historian, writer and editor based in North Carolina (yes, all of those things at once). She currently works as the senior editor at *The Counter*, a national publication that focuses on the politics, culture and business of food; there, her collaborative work on a series about how prison-produced food ends up in our food supply, 'Sourced from Inside', was a 2020 finalist for an Online Journalism Award. In 2020, she was awarded the James Beard Foundation Award for her foodways writing, the highest honour in American food writing. Her journalistic work appears in publications as diverse as *The New York Times*, the *Atlantic, Essence, Smithsonian, Longreads*, the *Nation, Vox* and *Vice*. She joined the University of Georgia Press as an editor at large, she's co-founder of the Carolina Abortion Fund and co-editor of *The Echoing Ida Collection*, an anthology of Black women and people writing about reproductive justice.

Tiffani Rozier is a freelance writer and podcast producer living in Phoenix, Arizona. She has an insatiable curiosity for people and their stories. For the past five years, she has been writing on topics such as food, wine, culture and hospitality. Her work has been published in *Cherry Bombe Magazine*, *Real Simple*, the *Philadelphia Inquirer* and more. She began producing and hosting an independent podcast called *Afros and Knives* in 2019. *Afros and Knives* is an interview series that amplifies Black women working in food and beverage, wine, and hospitality. It won its first award in 2020 and has featured guests like Fawn Weaver, Dr Jessica B. Harris, Osayi Endolyn, Korsha Wilson and Amber Mayfield. Most recently, she was the lead producer for *Black Material Geographies*, a newly minted podcast developed in conjunction with Stephen Satterfield, the host of Netflix's *High on the Hog*. She is passionate about discovering and shaping narratives in transformative and impactful ways.

ABOUT THE AUTHORS

Apoorva Sripathi is a Chennai-based writer, poet, anthropologist and also the co-founder and editor of the independent magazine *Cheese*. She has written for *Eater London*, *Vittles*, *Eaten*, *Pit* among other publications, and runs *shelf offering*, a food and culture newsletter.

Duron Chavis creates synergy between corporate social responsibility, public policy and traditional grassroots activism that builds community capacity for transformation. Transforming communities is an act that must take place through the community itself. By crafting collaborative approaches to collective impact, community work and personal evolution merge for sustainable systemic impact. From Happily Natural Day, to poverty mitigation, to urban agriculture, to racial equity, Chavis articulates the role cultural identity plays in sustainable community wellness. He challenges organisations and institutions to think outside of silos and to confront conversations of race and class courageously and authentically. Chavis serves as executive director of Happily Natural Day and co-founder of the Central Virginia Agrarian Community Land Trust.

Tambra Raye Stevenson, MPH, MA serves as the visionary leader of WANDA: Women Advancing Nutrition Dietetics and Agriculture, and she has been featured in the *Washington Post* and *Forbes*. Through education, advocacy and innovative approaches, WANDA is creating a pipeline and platform for women and girls of African descent to lead in building healthy sustainable communities from farm to health. Named as a 2020 Changemaker in the Food System by *Washington City Paper*, she is changing the narrative of women and girls in the food system working with government and media partners. She is also a patent holder and author of the WANDA bilingual children's picture book series encouraging young healthy eaters, readers and leaders. She serves on the Women in Toys, Licensing, and Entertainment's Diversity, Equity and Inclusion Committee.

Hassel Aviles has built a career in the hospitality and food-service industry for over two decades working primarily in restaurants, event production and entrepreneurship. In 2018, after years of struggling with mental illness and workplace trauma, Hassel was inspired to co-found Not 9 to 5, a non-profit that empowers service workers like herself. Five years later, Not 9 to 5 is now a global leader in mental health advocacy and education for the culinary and hospitality sector. Hassel has used her lived experience and social capital to create industry-specific solutions and support for workplace mental health in the hospitality industry and beyond. www.not9to5.org, @not9to5_, @hassel_aviles.

Vanessa Parish (she/her) is a Black Indigenous lesbian Chef that hosted the show *Tasting Our Roots* reaching over 10 million views and is on streaming platforms. Vanessa is a co-founder and director of the Queer Food Foundation, an organisation spotlighted by *NPR*, *Essence* and the James Beard Foundation. She continues to collaborate with Food Network, NBC, BET, AirBnB, Google, Access Hollywood and Blavity platforms. She has founded mutual aids, 'Brown Books for Brown Kids' and 'Tasty Tutelage'. She's been a contestant on *Chopped Sweets*, named Savage X Fenty's 2022 Change-maker, and is an *Eating Well* magazine correspondent. Vanessa is an advocate for Mental Health and Disability rights, Justice Reform and championing Queer Black Girl magic!

Abigail Koffler is the founder of *This Needs Hot Sauce*, a food newsletter and community established in 2017. She works in public relations for food and lifestyle brands, which involves a lot of strategy and snacking. Abigail is a freelance writer whose work has been published in *Food & Wine*, *Eater*, *Bustle* and more. She enjoys oyster happy hour and long walks. Abigail grew up in Queens and now lives in Brooklyn.

Lee Tran Lam is the editor of the *New Voices on Food* books and co-founder of Diversity In Food Media Australia. She's a freelance journalist based in Sydney (Eora), and has written for the *Guardian*, *SBS Food*, *Gourmet Traveller*, *Good Food* and *Eater*. Her podcasts include *The Unbearable Lightness of Being Hungry*, *Crunch Time*, *Culinary Archive* and *Should You Really Eat That? Time Out Sydney* ranked her as a 'Future Shaper' in Food and she once had a sandwich named after her.

Scott Alves Barton holds a PhD in Food Studies from NYU and is an Assistant Professor in Africana Studies at the University of Notre Dame. He had a twenty-five-year career as an executive chef and culinary educator. *Ebony* magazine named him one of the top twenty-five African American/Diaspora chefs. His research and publications focus on women's knowledge, the intersection of secular and sacred cuisine as a marker of identity politics, cultural heritage, political resistance and self-determination in Northeastern Brazil. Recent publications include 'Radical Moves from the Margins:

Enslaved Entertainments as Harvest Celebration in Northeastern Brazil' in *The Body Questions: Celebrating Flamenco's Tangled Roots*, and 'Food and Faith' in *Black Food: Stories, Art and Recipes from the African Diaspora*. Lynden Sculpture Garden, Milwaukee hosted Scott's recent exhibition honouring violence against Black bodies and ancestral worship, *Buried in the Heart: A Repast for Angels and Martyrs*. Scott is currently writing a companion manuscript, *Reckoning with Violence and Black Death: Repasts as Community Ritual*.

Selasie Dotse is the chef and owner of e le aɖe Test Kitchen, a fine dining pop-up concept offering a chef's table, supper club and other culinary experiences with an emphasis around African and Black stories throughout the Diaspora. Born in Accra, Ghana, and raised in the American South, Selasie started cooking at the age of six with their mother and aunties. After graduating with two degrees in culinary arts and food service management from Johnson & Wales University, they worked for several chefs and restaurants in Charlotte, North Carolina. They went on to work at several well-known and Michelin-rated restaurants in San Francisco and Oakland such as Avery, Lazy Bear, Mourad, SPQR and Hi Felicia. They are working on launching another pop-up called A Hard Pill to Swallow, which is a dinner series meant to acknowledge, showcase and support Black folks in the beverage, culinary, restaurant and hospitality industries and services. They live in Maryland.

Mavis-Jay Sanders is a chef who wakes up every morning and strives to leave the world a little better than it was yesterday. She is a social and racial equity activist that has dedicated her career to fighting for food justice in Black and low-income communities. In 2019, she was honoured as one of Star Chefs' New York Rising Stars. She is a James Beard Chef's Boot Camp alum, a mentor to the James Beard Foundation's Fellowship Program and a Chef's Collaborative scholar. She can also be found as an establishing board member of the Queer Food Foundation, on God's Love We Deliver's culinary counsel and in the Black Farmer Fund pilot community. Mavis-Jay's food focuses on celebrating Black American heritage, joy and a journey to reclaim Black food sovereignty. Most recently, she joined the team at Drive Change as director of Culinary Development and Education.

Chris Nigro is a Cook, Tranny, Writer exploring food as art. Currently: Cook at Moveable Feasts, which creates dinner-parties-in-a-box from James Beard and Michelin Award-winning restaurants. Napa Valley, New Zealand next.

Acknowledgements

My sincere gratitude and thanks to the sponsors and patrons who made the collection possible.

Notes

Foreword

1 Kevin Nance, 'The Spirit and the Strength: A Profile of Toni Morrison', *Poets & Writers Magazine*, November/December 2008, www.pw.org/content/the_spirit_and_the_strength_a_profile_of_toni_morrison
2 Joe Kobuthi, 'Food is Power', *Africa Is a Country*, africasacountry.com/2020/04/food-is-power

Columbusing Food and What It Looks Like

1 Sharon Otterman, 'A White Restaurateur Advertised "Clean" Chinese Food. Chinese-Americans Had Something to Say About It', *The New York Times*, 12 April 2019, www.nytimes.com/2019/04/12/nyregion/lucky-lees-nyc-chinese-food.html#:~:text=Haspel%27s%20decision%20to%20brand%20oher,not%20to%20mention%20otone%2Ddeaf.&text=This%20week%2C%20Ms.,icky%20after%20eating%20lo%20mein
2 Esther Tseng, 'How Lucky Lee's Could Have Gotten an "American Chinese" Restaurant Right', *Eater*, 10 April 2019, ny.eater.com/2019/4/10/18304897/lucky-lees-american-chinese-restaurant-controversy-nyc
3 'Chinese Restaurants in the US – Number of Businesses', *IBISWorld*, 22 June 2023, www.ibisworld.com/industry-statistics/number-of-businesses/chinese-restaurants-united-states/
4 Tyra Wu, 'The Sad Truth Behind Why There Are Over 40,000 Chinese Restaurants in America', *Spoon University*, 18 June 2016, spoonuniversity.

com/lifestyle/the-sad-truth-behind-why-there-are-over-40000-chinese-restaurants-in-america
5 Maura Judkis, 'Hawaiian poke has never been trendier. But the mainland is ruining it', *The Washington Post*, 27 July 2017, www.washingtonpost.com/goingoutguide/the-poke-bowls-swarming-dc-are-tasty-but-dont-call-them-authentic-hawaiian-food/2017/07/26/8de42e6c-6bf3-11e7-96ab-5f38140b38cc_story.html
6 Ashok Selvam, 'Chicago's Aloha Poke Faces Boycott Over Hawaiian Cultural Appropriation Claims', *Eater*, 30 July 2018, chicago.eater.com/2018/7/30/17629738/aloha-poke-cease-desist-kanaka-hawaii-boycott-levy
7 Facebook post by Aloha Poke Co., 30 July 2018, www.facebook.com/Alohapokeco/posts/2162695770681984
8 Ashok Selvam, 'Aloha Poke Co. Apologizes to Native Hawaiians', *Eater*, 30 July 2018, chicago.eater.com/2018/7/30/17631154/aloha-poke-response-boycott-leis-poke-stop-anchorage-alaska
9 Facebook post by Kalama O Ka Aina, 28 July 2018, www.facebook.com/kalama.okaaina/videos/10214956936069082/. This link is no longer active.
10 Walker MacMurdo, 'Kooks Serves Pop-Up Breakfast Burritos With Handmade Tortillas Out of a Food Cart on Cesar Chavez', *Willamette Week*, 16 May 2017, www.wweek.com/uncategorized/2017/05/16/kooks-serves-pop-up-breakfast-burritos-with-handmade-tortillas-out-of-a-food-cart-on-cesar-chavez/

The Food Talent Pipeline

1 Elizabeth Grieco, 'Newsroom employees are less diverse than US workers overall', Pew Research Center, 2 November 2018, www.pewresearch.org/fact-tank/2018/11/02/newsroom-employees-are-less-diverse-than-u-s-workers-overall/
2 'ASNE's 2018 diversity survey results reflect low participation but encouraging shifts', ASNE, 2018, www.asne.org/diversity-survey-2018
3 Amy Fleming, 'The geography of taste: how our food preferences are formed', *The Guardian*, 3 September 2013.
4 Stephanie K. Baer, 'The Editor of Bon Appétit Is Resigning After a Photo of Him in Brownface Resurfaced', *BuzzFeed News*, 10 June 2020,

www.buzzfeednews.com/article/skbaer/bon-appetit-adam-rapoport-brown-face-racism

5 Hannah Beech, 'Eating Thai Fruit Demands Serious Effort but Offers Sublime Reward', *The New York Times*, 22 June 2020, www.nytimes.com/2020/06/22/world/asia/bangkok-thailand-fruit-durian.html

6 David Folkenflik, 'People of color at "New York Times" get lower ratings in job reviews, union says', *NPR*, 23 August 2022, www.npr.org/2022/08/23/1118817023/new-york-times-race-employees-job-review-union

Un Asiento En La Mesa

1 'Anthony Bourdain on Illegal Immigrant Labor in U.S. Kitchens', *Houston Press*, 19 December 2007, www.houstonpress.com/restaurants/anthony-bourdain-on-illegal-immigrant-labor-in-us-kitchens-6438849

'It's too spicy' and Other Such Bullshit

1 'New report reveals eight in ten chefs suffer from poor mental health', *Nestle*, 15 May 2019, www.nestle.co.uk/en-gb/media/pressreleases/new-report-reveals-eight-in-ten-chefs-suffer-from-poor-mental-health#:~:text=New%20report%20reveals%20eight%20in%20ten%20chefs%20suffer%20from%20poor%20mental%20health,-Share%20this%20page&text=In%20a%20

The Things We Could Not Swallow

1 Olivier Jolliet, 'Small Changes in Diet Could Help You Live Healthier, More Sustainably', School of Public Health University of Michigan, 19 August 2021, sph.umich.edu/news/2021posts/small-changes-in-diet-could-help-you-live-healthier-more-sustainably.html

Inheritance

1 Apoorva Sripathi, 'The cultural politics of olfaction', *shelf offering*, 31 August 2020, shelfoffering.substack.com/p/the-cultural-politics-of-olfaction

2 G. Arunima, 'Being vegetarian, the Hindu way', *Economic and Political Weekly*, 18 April 2014, www.epw.in/blogs/g-arunima/being-vegetarian-hindu-way.html

3 'Religion and food' from Religion in India, Tolerance and Segregation, Pew Research Center, 29 June 2021, www.pewresearch.org/religion/2021/06/29/religion-and-food/
4 Chitrita Banerji, 'Feeding the Gods', in *The Hour of the Goddess*, Penguin Books India, Delhi, 2006.
5 C. Sathyamala, 'Meat-eating in India: Whose food, whose politics, and whose rights?', *Policy Futures in Education*, 17: 7, 2018.
6 P. Sainath, 'And you thought it's only about farmers?', *PARI*, 10 December 2020, ruralindiaonline.org/en/articles/and-you-thought-its-only-about-farmers/

Still Standing

1 Julie Besonen, 'For Richmond, a Compelling New Chapter', *The New York Times*, 26 December 2022, www.nytimes.com/2022/12/26/travel/richmond-virginia-african-american-culture.html
2 'Monument Avenue, VA Housing Market', Redfin, www.redfin.com/neighborhood/87321/VA/Richmond/Monument-Avenue/housing-market
3 'Formerly Redlined Areas of Richmond Are Going Green', Chesapeake Bay Foundation, 15 September 2020, www.cbf.org/blogs/save-the-bay/2020/09/formerly-redlined-areas-of-richmond-are-going-green.html
4 'Mapping Life Expectancy', Virginia Commonwealth University's Center on Society and Health, 26 September 2016, societyhealth.vcu.edu/work/the-projects/mapping-life-expectancy.html#gsc.tab=0
5 Antonio Moore, 'Who Owns Almost All America's land?', *Inequality.org*, 15 February 2016, inequality.org/research/owns-land/#:~:text=White%20Americans%2C%20by%20comparison%2C%20own,worth%20of%20over%20%241%20trillion

Serving Up Sisterhood

1 Harsha Walia, 'Decolonizing together: Moving beyond a politics of solidarity toward a practice of decolonization', *Briarpatch Magazine*, 1 January 2012, briarpatchmagazine.com/articles/view/decolonizing-together#:~:text=%E2%80%9CSolidarity%20is%20not%20the%20same,and%20just%20as%20easily%20withdrawn

NOTES

2 The Kitchen Sisters, Jamie York, 'The Club From Nowhere: Cooking for Civil Rights', *NPR*, 4 March 2005, www.npr.org/2005/03/04/4509998/the-club-from-nowhere-cooking-for-civil-rights
3 Keisha N. Blain, 'Fannie Lou Hamer's Dauntless Fight for Black Americans' Right to Vote', *Smithsonian Magazine*, 20 August 2020, www.smithsonianmag.com/history/fannie-lou-hamers-dauntless-fight-for-black-americans-right-vote-180975610/
4 Paula Giddings, *When and Where I Enter: The Impact of Black Women on Race and Sex in America*, William Morrow, New York, 1984.
5 Semhar Araia, www.semhararaia.com/speaking
6 Audre Lorde, 'Eye to eye: Black Women, Hatred, and Anger', in *Sister Outsider*, Crossing Press, Berkeley, 1984.
7 Maya Angelou, *The Complete Collected Poems of Maya Angelou*, Random House, New York, 1994.

Neuro Spicy

1 Avery Harris-Grey, 'What is the DiSC Di Type?', DiSCprofiles.com, www.discprofiles.com/disc-di-type/#:~:text=People%20whose%20DiSC%C2%AE%20profile,viewed%20as%20dynamic%20and%20outspoken
2 'ACE Screening Clinical Workflows, ACEs and Toxic Stress Risk Assessment Algorithm, and ACE-Associated Health Conditions: For Pediatrics and Adults', acesaware.org, April 2020, www.acesaware.org/wp-content/uploads/2019/12/ACE-Clinical-Workflows-Algorithms-and-ACE-Associated-Health-Conditions.pdf
3 Erica M. Webster, 'The Impact of Adverse Childhood Experiences on Health and Development in Young Children', *Global Pediatric Health*, 2022. doi: 10.1177/2333794X221078708. PMID: 35237713; PMCID: PMC888293
4 Twitter post by @NomeDaBarbarian via PingThread, 15 May 2022, www.pingthread.com/thread/1525665010466164736
5 James Hansen, 'New Platform Black Book Aims to Redistribute Power and Wealth in Food', *Eater*, 7 July 2020, london.eater.com/2020/7/7/21315821/black-book-2020-food-media-events-zoe-adjonyoh-anna-sulan-masing-frankie

6 Young, Susan et al., 'Females with ADHD: An expert consensus statement taking a lifespan approach providing guidance for the identification and treatment of attention-deficit/hyperactivity disorder in girls and women', *BMC Psychiatry*, 12 August 2020, doi: 10.1186/s12888-020-02707-9, pmc.ncbi.nlm.nih.gov/articles/PMC7422602/

7 D. E. Attoe, E. A. Climie, 'Miss. Diagnosis: A Systematic Review of ADHD in Adult Women', *Journal of Attention Disorders*, 27: 7, pp. 645–57, 2023. doi: 10.1177/10870547231161533. Epub 2023 Mar 30. PMID: 36995125; PMCID: PMC10173330.

8 Claire Sibonney, 'With a Diagnosis at Last, Black Women with ADHD Start Healing', KFF Health News, 20 July 2021, kffhealthnews.org/news/article/black-women-adhd-attention-deficit-hyperactivity-disorder-underdiagnosed/#:~:text=Already%20subject%20to%20unique%20discrimination,mistaken%20for%20laziness%20or%20defiance

Psychological Safety in Hospitality and Beyond

1 'Human Capital Benchmarking Report', The Society for Human Resources Management, 8 August 2016, www.shrm.org/topics-tools/news/shrm-benchmarking-report-4129-average-cost-per-hire

2 Alexandra Jones, 'The restaurant labor shortage: how we got here and a 2023 update', *Open Table*, 2023, restaurant.opentable.com/resources/restaurant-labor-shortage

3 Jessica Reimer and Sarah Zorn, 'What is the Average Restaurant Profit Margin in Canada? Tips for Benchmarking and Optimizing', *Toast*, pos.toasttab.com/ca/blog/on-the-line/average-restaurant-profit-margin

4 Dr Jarek Conrad, 'The Impact of Work on Mental Health', UKG Workforce Institute, 2 February 2023, www.ukg.com/blog/workforce-institute/the-impact-of-work-on-mental-health

5 Donald Sull, Charles Sull, Ben Zweig, 'Toxic Culture is Driving The Great Resignation', *MIT Sloan Management Review*, 11 January 2022, sloanreview.mit.edu/article/toxic-culture-is-driving-the-great-resignation/

6 'New Mental Health Cost Calculator Shows Why Investing in Mental Health is Good for Business', National Safety Council, 13 May 2021,

www.nsc.org/newsroom/new-mental-health-cost-calculator-demonstrates-why

7 Natasha Tamiru, 'Team dynamics: Five keys to building effective teams', *Think with Google*, June 2023, business.google.com/uk/think/future-of-marketing/five-dynamics-effective-team/

8 J. Borenstien, 'Stigma, prejudice and discrimination against people with mental illness', *American Psychiatric Association*, August 2020, www.psychiatry.org/patients-families/stigma-and-discrimination

9 Jaimie L. Gradus, Tammy Jiang, Katherine M. Keyes, Gonzalo Martínez-Alés, 'The Recent Rise of Suicide Mortality in the United States', *Annual Review of Public Health*, 27 October 2021, www.annualreviews.org/doi/pdf/10.1146/annurev-publhealth-051920-123206

Was Anthony Bourdain Wrong About Vegan Food?

1 Justin Wm. Moyer, 'Anthony Bourdain defends immigrants, shreds Trump and lazy culinary school kids', *Washington Post*, 30 October 2015, www.washingtonpost.com/news/morning-mix/wp/2015/10/30/anthony-bourdain-defends-immigrants-shreds-trump-and-lazy-culinary-school-kids/

Why Black Spaces Are Needed in an Industry That Refuses to Change

1 Instagram post by Ashtin Berry @thecollectress, 7 May 2021, www.instagram.com/p/COjgkJxL9ZA/

Unbound is a publisher which champions bold, unexpected books.

We give readers the opportunity to support books directly, so our authors are empowered to take creative risks and write the books they really want to write. We help readers to discover new writing they won't find anywhere else.

We are building a community in which authors engage directly with people who love what they do. It's a place where readers and writers can connect with and support one another, enjoy unique experiences and benefits, and make books that matter.

This book is in your hands because readers made it possible. Everyone who pledged their support is listed below. Join them by visiting unbound.com and supporting a book today.

Abby
Andrea Borgen Abdallah
Ed Accura
Ama Acheampong-Mensah
Martha Adam-Bushell
Yaa Adansi-Pipim
Liz Adelanwa
Stephen Adjaidoo
Sheryl Agyemang and Sarah Joy Dawoud
Jane Aiello
Kathleen Ainslie

SUPPORTERS

Sae Akine
Imad Alarnab
Beverley Allen
Tessa Allingham
Bridget Anderson
Sarah Anderson
Stephen Anderson
Hillary Ann
Lucy Antal
M Ardebili
Johannes J. Arens
Camilla Arnold
Dare Arowe
Arvin
Frankie Asante
Yesenia Avila
Hassel Aviles
John Backhouse
John Bailey
Julia Bainbridge
Jade Baker
Adiyatu Sambu Balde
Melissa Baldino
Katie Barasch
Scott Barton
Aneesha Batavia
Tess Beck
Alexandrea Becker
Will Beckett
Indie Beedie
Ixta Belfrage

Rachel Belward
Dr. Jennifer Benjamin
Annie Bennett
Mary Bennett
Natalie Bennett
Phillip Bennett-Richards
Sarah Bentley
Lindsey Berk
Harshika Bhatt
Uli Bilke
Shell Bird
Rosie Birkett
Meera Bissoondeeal
Wanda Blake
Jennifer Blundell
Joanne Boal
Kristine Bolander
Vanessa Bolosier
Ginny Bonifacino
Hattie Bowden-Howl
Lauren Bowes
Elizabeth Bowman
Jackson Boxer
Julie Boyles
Mark Breen
Laura Brehaut
Colette Brown
Isabella Brown
Jessica Brown
Marie Brown
Martin Brown

SUPPORTERS

Brian Browne
Craig Bullions
Chris Bulow of Salute The Pig
Regan Burns
Brian Burrell
Robin Busch-Wheaton
Peter Butler
Claire Buysse
Theodora Cadbury
Lindsay Cameron
Francesca Caracciolo
Sloane Carvell
Chai (he/him)
Ben Chandler
Pei Chang
Benjamin Chiou
Chrissy, Ian, Christopher, Anna
Lisa Christensen
Jeanie Chunn
Madeleine Cirdei
Amanda Clarke
Elizabeth Clarke
Amy Cleary
Mary Cleaver
Felicity Cloake
Sheena Mushett Cole
Claire Coleman
Camylle Coley
Sarah Cooke
Michelle Coomber
Canela Corrales
Brianne Cortright
Brona Cosgrave
Dana Cowin
Andy Cowley
Julian Crowe
Sue Currie
Bianca Datta
Amanda David
Emily Davies
Rachel Davies
Laura Davis
Cheryl Day
Jasmin De Freitas
Lucy Dearlove
Sophie de Graft-Johnson
Patric Ffrench Devitt
Renée Devonish
Liz Dexter
Craig Dickson
Christie Dietz
Samantha Dodd
Phoebe Dodds
Cristina Dominguez
Ellie Doney
Siobhan Dooley
Parrus Doshi
Raeghn Draper
Catherine Drew
Charlotte Druckman

SUPPORTERS

E.F.
Seraphina Edelmann
Eden
EGP
June Ellerby
Cathy Erway
Jessica Esa
Reinhard Eschbach
Bunmi Esho
Cada Fabian
Juliana Falkenstein
Fiona Farnsworth
Finbarr Farragher
Francesca Farris
Maia Fernandez
Sally Fincher
Kathleen Finlay
Anna Fisher
Molly Flatt
Simon Floodgate
Jazmine Foote
Jean Forbes
Alicia Fourie
Ceri Fowler
Clara Frain-Atallah
Lena Frain-Atallah
Steph Francis
Rebekah Galang
Alex Garza
Daniela Garza
Claire Genevieve

Will Georgi
Daniele Gibney
Abby Gilbert
Rina Gill
Andrew Gillman
Sally Gleeson
Sasha Göbbels
Lisa Gobmeier
Caoimhe Good
Ristina Gooden
Lizzi Gorman
Huw Gott
Helen Graves
Rachel Green
Aliya Gulamani
Sannah Gulamani
Elisa Gurule
Karena Halvorssen
Daniel Hammond
James Hansen
Georgia Harber
Becca Harper-Day
Carmen Harris
Shayna Harris
Ruth Harrison
Sarah Haswell
Jack Hawthorn
Amy Hayward
Clare Heal
Melissa Hemsley
Roisin Henman-Kyle

SUPPORTERS

Elaine Hill
Lucy Hinnie
Grace Hochheimer
Marten Hoekstra
John Holland
Robin Homonoff
Francesca Hopkins
Anna Himali Howard
Nathalie Hudson
Chris Hulbert
Andrew Hunt
Sarah Hunt
Laura Hurley
Philippa Illsley
Lin James
JoAnn Janjigian
Camilla Jarvis
Joanna Jedrasiak
Benjamin Jennings
Kristin Jensen
Mark Jewell
Krish Jeyakumar
Gilbert Johnson
Laura Johnson
Harriet Jordan
Alice Julier
Sana Kadri
Shikha Kaiwar
Justine Kanter
Petros Karatsareas
Katie & Robyn

Sarah Keech
Cary Kelly
Tess Kelly
Adrienne Katz Kennedy
Alicia Kennedy
Eleanor Kenny
Rachel Ketola
Dan Kieran
Gabrielle Kirby
Kalamata's Kitchen
Laura Kitchings
Kamillah Knight
Bernd Horst Knöller
Gavan Knox
Georgina Koch
Karen and Neil Koffler
Adam Kowit
Rachel Krupa
Niketa Kumar
Emily Kyne
Frank Lampen
Mimi Lan
Tiffany Langston
Laurie Larimer
Zoe Yu Tung Law
Josephine Lawrence
Patrice Lawrence
Nigella Lawson
Robin Leach
Grace Lee
Diane Leedham

SUPPORTERS

Gabrielle Lenart
Natalia Levey
Amina Appiah Lewis
Liz
Nikki Lloyd-Brown
Cara Lopez
Diana Lopez
Susan Low
Lindsey Lustig
Jenny Lynch
Lauren M
Siobhan Mackenzie
Marie-Anne Mackie
Jessica Madieros
Reena Makwana
Gita Malhotra
Anela Malik
Gurpreet Mann
Nadirah Mansour
Theda Markarian
Daniel Marsh
Jessica Marston
Anna Masing
Laura Mason
Jo Massie
Melissa Mazzeo
MC
Anne McBride
Nancie S. McDermott
Carolyn McGill
Carole McIntosh

Christine Mckenna-tirella
Hetty McKinnon
Aidan McQuade
Emily Rose McRae
Russell McRae
Marie Merillat
Emily Meseck
Daniela Michanie
Michminx
Mark Middleton
Natalia Middleton
Tammy Milbury
Faith Miller
Katherine Miller
Klancy Miller
Nic Miller
Tara Christina Miller
Deborah Millington
Lora Lea Misterly
Harry Mistry
Sarah Mitchell
Talia Moore
Kate Morrison
Michelle Morrison
Lucy Munene
Carlo Navato
Sasha Nemeckova
Miranda Schiller Neuhauser
Laura Nickoll
Nicole Noble
Not 9 To 5 Organization

SUPPORTERS

Nuzha Nuseibeh
Ray O
Sam Oladele
Naomi Oppenheim
Larry Ossei-Mensah
Affiong Osuchukwu
Laura Ovenden
Elektra Owen
Dawn Padmore
Peter Panda
Jessica Parrish
Dan Pashman
Toddy Peters
Brian Petro
Helen Pine
Ryan Pintado-Vertner
Nigel Planer
Caroline Plante
Niko Plaskasovitis
Lydia Pluckrose
Clair Poletti
Giulia Polito
Beki Pope
Pippa Postgate
Liz Potts
Louisa Pratt
Katherine Price
Liz Price
Miriam Price
Tara Pritchard
Jerry Pura

Stephanie Rachmeler
Karishma Rafferty
Lisa Raftery
Meghan Reid
Kerry-Jo Reilly
Andrea Reusing
Eleanor Reynolds
Lucy Riseborough
Katherine Riva
Vannessa Rivera
Tony Rodd
Danielle Aquino Roithmayr
Jenny Rollo
Branco Rood
Ali Rosen
Holly Rosenthal
Anna Route
Emily Saladino
Elizabeth Salib
Anne-Maria Salmon
Thea Sandall
Stephanie Fine Sasse
Molly Schemper
Barbara Segall
Jess Sells
Dick Selwood
Kate Shannon
Timothy Sheard
Terry Tidridge Shemansky
Maureen Shenton

SUPPORTERS

Nikesh Shukla
Laurel Sills
Elsa Da Silva
Lara Silveira
Gemma Simko
Dr. Kathryn Sisa
Liam Skillen
Mieke Smit
Chris Smith
Grace Smith
Rachel Smith
Elizabeth Sowula
Perteet Spencer
Denise Spencer-Walker
Sarah Spenser
Nicholas St. Hill
Charity Stafford
Rick Steele
Gabriela Steinke
Rachel Stella
Polly Stephens
Melissa Stewart
Whitney Stewart
Claire Stimpson
Theodore Stone
Matilda Streatfeild
Miriam Streiman
Shaun Strohmer
Pauline Subran
Yuko Sugimoto
Aisling O Sullivan

Elaine Swan
Tait Sye
Michael Szczerban
Daniel Tagg
Hannah Tappis
Aziz Tarkhan
Abby Taylor
Milli Taylor
Sujata Tejwani
Julie Tharalson
Cathy Thomas
Ben Thompson
Liz Thompson
Ian Thompson-Corr
Eva Thorne
Kate Tilbury
Ruth Till
Valerie Tirella
Torrie
Tríona
Camila Troughton
Ai-Ling Truong
Tina Tse
Paul Turkson
Allison Turner
Hannah Turner
Lewis Turner
Laura Twining
Fatih Uzuner
Aaron Vallance
Miranda Vega

SUPPORTERS

Bart-Jan Veldhuizen
Isabela Vera
Pen Vogler
Georgina Vye
Shawn Walker-Smith
Kenza Walthour
Chee Lup Wan
Hillary Wasserman
Annie Watson
Elisabeth Weiman
Christianne Wilhelmson
Zoe Williams

Johanna Wilson
Wendy Wong
Charlotte Wood
Dawn Woodward
Steve Woodward
Gavin Wren
Aga Wypychowska
Lisa Yadao
Nathan Young
Charlene Yum
Helen Zaltzman
Zola